Beat the Forex: 50 Strategies Explained

Allfonso Borello

Villlaggio Publishing Ltd

CONTENTS

LESS IS MORE IN FOREX: DITCH THE SYSTEM OVERLOAD, MASTER A FEW FOR TRADING SUCCESS

Using as many systems as possible is not an absolute imperative to balance in Forex trading. In fact, it can be counterproductive and lead to overtrading and poor decision-making.

There are a few reasons why using multiple systems can be problematic:

Increased complexity: Each trading system has its own set of rules and parameters. Trying to keep track of and manage multiple systems can be complex and time-consuming, especially for beginner traders.

Conflicting signals: Different trading systems may generate conflicting signals, which can lead to confusion and indecision. This can result in missed opportunities or poor trade entries and exits.

Overtrading: Using multiple systems can lead to overtrading, as traders may feel the need to constantly monitor the markets and make trades in order to justify the time and effort spent on learning and managing multiple systems. This can lead to excessive risk-taking and poor trading outcomes.

Instead of using as many systems as possible, it is better to focus on developing a deep understanding of a few well-chosen systems that are appropriate for your trading style and risk tolerance. This will allow you to trade with greater confidence and discipline, and will ultimately lead to better trading results.

In addition to the above, there are a few other things to consider when choosing a trading system:

Track record: Look for a trading system with a proven track record of profitability. This does not guarantee future success, but it is a good starting point.

Simplicity: Choose a trading system that is easy to understand and implement. The more complex a system is, the more likely you are to make mistakes.

Risk management: Make sure the trading system has a built-in risk management strategy. This will help you to protect your capital from losses.

Once you have chosen a trading system, it is important to paper trade it for a period of time before risking real money. This will allow you to test the system and make sure that it is working as expected.

CAN WILLPOWER HELP?

Yes, willpower can help in Forex trading, but it is important to understand its limitations and use it effectively. Here's how willpower can be beneficial in Forex trading:

Control emotions: Forex trading can be emotionally challenging, especially during losing streaks or when faced with large market movements. Willpower can help you to stay calm and disciplined, and avoid making impulsive or emotional decisions.

Stick to a trading plan: Developing a trading plan is essential for success in Forex trading. Willpower can help you to follow your trading plan consistently, even when it means taking small losses or missing out on potential profits.

Manage risk: Risk management is a crucial aspect of Forex trading. Willpower can help you to resist the temptation to overtrade or take on excessive risk, which can lead to significant losses.

However, it is important to recognize that willpower is not a limitless resource. It can be depleted over time, especially when faced with ongoing challenges or setbacks. Therefore, it is important to use willpower strategically and in combination with other tools and techniques to improve your trading performance.

Here Are Some Tips For Using Willpower Effectively In Forex Trading:

Set realistic goals: Don't try to achieve too much too soon. Start with small, achievable goals and gradually increase them as you gain experience and confidence.

Break down large tasks into smaller ones: This will make them seem less daunting and more manageable.

Focus on the process, not the outcome: Don't get too caught up in the results of your trades. Instead, focus on the process of making good trading decisions and executing your trades properly.

Take breaks: It is important to take breaks from trading, especially when you are feeling stressed or fatigued. This will help you to conserve your willpower and avoid burnout.

Reward yourself: When you achieve your goals, reward yourself for your hard work. This will help to reinforce positive behavior and keep you motivated.

Remember that willpower is just one tool that can contribute to your success in Forex trading. It is important to also develop a solid understanding of the market, effective trading strategies, and sound risk management principles.

HOW MUCH SHOULD YOU INVEST?

How much you should invest in Forex trading depends on several factors, including:

Your financial situation: Consider your overall financial goals, risk tolerance, and disposable income when determining how much to invest in Forex.

Your trading strategy: Some trading strategies, such as scalping, require a smaller account balance compared to swing trading or position trading.

The leverage you are using: Leverage can magnify your profits and losses. Be sure to understand the risks associated with leverage before using it.

As a general rule of thumb, it is recommended to start with a small account balance, such as $1,000 or less, until you gain experience and confidence in your trading abilities. This will help you to limit your risk and avoid large losses.

DOES IT MAKE A DIFFERENCE?

Yes, the amount you invest can make a difference in your Forex trading results. Here are a few reasons why:

Larger account balance: A larger account balance allows you to trade larger position sizes, which can lead to larger profits. However, it also exposes you to greater risk.

Compounding: Compounding is the effect of earning interest on your interest. The larger your account balance, the more interest you will earn, which can lead to exponential growth over time.

Margin calls: If you are using leverage, you may be subject to margin calls if your account balance falls below a certain level. This can force you to close your positions at a loss.

It is important to remember that Forex trading is a risky endeavor, and there is no guarantee of success. Do not invest more money than you can afford to lose.

Here are some tips for managing your risk in Forex trading:

Use stop-loss orders: Stop-loss orders automatically close your positions when the market reaches a predetermined price level, limiting your losses.

Don't overtrade: Overtrading can lead to excessive risk-taking and poor decision-making. Trade only when you have a high-probability trading opportunity.

Manage your emotions: Forex trading can be emotionally

challenging. It is important to stay calm and disciplined, and avoid making impulsive or emotional decisions.

Remember, the key to successful Forex trading is not to make a lot of money quickly, but to consistently make small profits over time. This can be achieved by using sound risk management principles and a well-developed trading plan. All said, let's get to it.

| 1. TREND FOLLOWING

| Buy when the market is trending up, sell when trending down. | Easy to understand, can be profitable in strong trends. | Can be difficult to identify trends, can be whipsawed in choppy markets. | 1-2% of account | 2-3 ATR | 1-2 ATR | Trending pairs, e.g., EUR/USD, GBP/USD | Follow the trend |

Interpretation

1. Trend Following Strategy:

The trend following strategy is a simple, yet effective trading approach that seeks to profit from market trends.

The basic principle is to buy when the market is trending up, and sell when it is trending down.

Advantages:

   The strategy is easy to understand and apply.
   It can be profitable, especially in strong and sustained trends.

Disadvantages:

   Identifying valid trends can be challenging, especially for beginner traders.
   The strategy can lead to whipsawing, where traders frequently enter and exit trades with small profits or

losses in choppy market conditions.

It requires a certain level of risk tolerance, as traders may need to hold positions for an extended period to capture significant profits.

2. Risk Management:

Account Allocation:
Allocate 1-2% of your trading account to each trade.

Stop Loss Placement:
Place a stop loss order 2-3 ATR (Average True Range) away from the entry price.

Profit Taking:
Take profit at a target that is 1-2 ATR away from the entry price.

3. Suitable Market Conditions:

The trend following strategy is best suited for trending markets, such as the EUR/USD and GBP/USD currency pairs.
It is less effective in choppy or sideways markets.

4. Trading Rule:

Follow the Trend:
Identify an uptrend or downtrend using technical indicators or price action patterns.
Enter a long trade (buy) when the market is trending up and a short trade (sell) when trending down.

ATR EXPLAINED

The Average True Range (ATR) is a technical indicator that measures the volatility of a market. It is calculated by taking the average of the true range values over a specified period, typically 14 trading days. The true range is defined as the greatest of the following three values:

The current high minus the current low

The absolute value of the current high minus the previous close

The absolute value of the current low minus the previous close

Significance of ATR:

1. Volatility Assessment:

The ATR provides a quantitative measure of market volatility.

Higher ATR values indicate higher volatility, while lower values indicate lower volatility.

Traders can use the ATR to assess the risk associated with a particular market or trading instrument.

2. Stop Loss Placement:

The ATR is commonly used to determine appropriate stop loss levels.

Placing a stop loss order a certain number of ATRs away from the entry price helps traders limit their risk in case of adverse price movements.

3. Position Sizing:

The ATR can also be used to determine appropriate position sizes.

Traders may adjust their position size based on the ATR to manage their risk exposure.

4. Trailing Stop:

The ATR can be incorporated into trailing stop strategies.

A trailing stop is an order that automatically adjusts its stop loss level as the market moves in a favorable direction.

The ATR can be used to determine the distance between the current market price and the trailing stop.

By incorporating the ATR into their trading strategies, traders can better manage risk, determine appropriate position sizes, and potentially improve their trading performance.

| 2. COUNTER-TREND TRADING

| Buy when the market is oversold, sell when overbought. | Can be profitable in mean-reverting markets. | Can be difficult to identify overbought/oversold conditions, can be whipsawed in trending markets. | 1% of account | 1-2 ATR | 1-2 ATR | Range-bound pairs, e.g., EUR/JPY, GBP/JPY | Oversold/overbought conditions|

Counter-trend trading is a strategy that involves buying when the market is experiencing an oversold condition, and selling when the market is in an overbought condition. This strategy can be profitable in mean-reverting markets, where the market tends to move back to its average price after a period of time. However, it can be difficult to identify overbought and oversold conditions, and traders can be whipsawed in trending markets.

To implement this strategy, traders should use 1% of their account balance for each trade. They should also use stop-loss orders that are set 1-2 ATRs (average true range) away from the entry price, and take-profit orders that are set 1-2 ATRs away from the entry price.

Counter-trend trading is best suited for range-bound pairs, such as EUR/JPY and GBP/JPY. These pairs tend to move in a back-and-forth motion, which makes them ideal for counter-trend trading.

Traders should use technical indicators to identify overbought and oversold conditions. Some popular indicators include the relative strength index (RSI), the stochastic oscillator, and the Bollinger Bands.

| 3. SCALPING

| Buy and sell very quickly, taking small profits on each trade. | Can be profitable in volatile markets. | Requires fast reaction times, can be stressful. | 0.5-1% of account | 10-20 pips | 10-20 pips | Volatile pairs, e.g., EUR/USD, GBP/USD | High volatility periods |

Scalping is a short-term trading strategy that involves buying and selling a currency pair very quickly, typically within a few minutes or even seconds. The goal is to make small profits on each trade, rather than holding onto a position for a longer period of time.

Scalping can be profitable in volatile markets, where there is a lot of movement in the price of a currency pair. However, it requires fast reaction times and can be stressful, as traders need to be constantly monitoring the market and making quick decisions.

To scalp effectively, traders typically use technical analysis to identify trends and patterns in the market. They may also use specific trading indicators or automated trading systems to help them make decisions.

Scalping can be a profitable strategy for experienced traders who are willing to put in the time and effort to learn how to do it effectively. However, it is not a suitable strategy for beginner traders, as it requires a lot of skill and experience.

Here Are Some Key Points To Keep In Mind About Scalping:

Risk: Scalping is a high-risk trading strategy, as traders are taking multiple trades in a short period of time. This can lead to significant losses if the trader is not careful.

Reward: The potential rewards of scalping can be high, as traders can make multiple profits in a short period of time. However, the profits are typically small, so traders need to make a lot of trades to make a significant profit.

Time: Scalping is a time-consuming trading strategy, as traders need to be constantly monitoring the market and making quick decisions. This can be difficult for traders who have other commitments, such as a job or family.

Skill: Scalping is a difficult trading strategy to learn. It requires a lot of skill and experience to be successful. Beginner traders should not attempt to scalp until they have a good understanding of the market and have developed a consistent trading strategy.

| 4. DAY TRADING

| Buy and sell within the same day, closing all positions before the market closes. | Can be profitable in trending markets. | Requires a lot of time and attention, can be stressful. | 1-2% of account | 2-3 ATR | 1-2 ATR | Trending pairs, e.g., EUR/USD, GBP/USD | During the day |

Day trading is a trading strategy that involves buying and selling financial instruments within the same trading day, with the intent of capitalizing on short-term price movements. Day traders typically close all their positions before the market closes, avoiding the risk of overnight price movements.

Advantages:

Profitable in Trending Markets: Day trading can be profitable in trending markets, where prices are moving consistently in one direction. By buying and selling in line with the trend, day traders can potentially profit from significant price movements.

Disadvantages:

Requires a Lot of Time and Attention: Day trading requires a lot of time and attention, as traders need to constantly monitor the market and make quick decisions. This can be stressful and demanding, especially for those who are not experienced in trading.

Risk Management:

1-2% of Account: Day traders should risk no more than 1-2% of their trading account on any single trade. This helps to limit losses and preserve capital.

Trade Management:

2-3 ATR: Day traders should use a stop loss of 2-3 ATR (Average True Range) to protect their profits and limit losses.

1-2 ATR: Day traders should take profit at 1-2 ATR to secure their profits and avoid giving them back to the market.

Suitable Markets:

Trending Pairs: Day trading is best suited for trending currency pairs, such as EUR/USD and GBP/USD, as these pairs tend to exhibit consistent price movements.

Trading Hours:

During the Day: Day trading is typically done during the day, when the market is most active and there is the greatest liquidity.

| 5. SWING TRADING

| Buy and sell over a period of days or weeks, holding positions for multiple days or weeks. | Can be profitable in trending markets. | Requires patience, can be difficult to identify swing points. | 2-3% of account | 3-5 ATR | 2-3 ATR | Trending pairs, e.g., EUR/USD, GBP/USD | During a trend |

Swing trading is a trading strategy where positions are held for multiple days or weeks, with the aim of capturing larger market moves. It involves buying and selling financial instruments such as stocks, Forex, or commodities over a period of days or weeks, rather than making short-term trades within a single day.

Key Points

1. Timeframe: Swing traders hold positions for multiple days or weeks, unlike day traders who close their positions within the same day. This longer timeframe allows swing traders to capture larger market trends and fluctuations.

2. Market Trend: Swing trading can be profitable in trending markets, where the price of an asset is moving in a consistent direction over time. Traders aim to identify and trade with the trend, buying when the price is rising and selling when the price is falling.

3. Patience and Timing: Swing trading requires patience and the ability to wait for the right trading opportunities. Traders need

to identify swing points, which are the highs and lows in a trend, and enter positions at these points. This can be challenging and requires careful analysis of market data and technical indicators.

4. Risk Management: Swing traders typically allocate a small portion of their trading account, around 2-3%, to each trade. They use stop-loss orders to limit potential losses and manage risk effectively.

5. Average True Range (ATR): The ATR is a technical indicator that measures market volatility. Swing traders often use the ATR to determine their profit targets and stop-loss levels. A higher ATR indicates higher volatility, which can lead to larger potential profits but also greater risk.

6. Trading Pairs: Swing traders often focus on trending currency pairs in the Forex market, such as EUR/USD and GBP/USD. These pairs are known for their strong trends and liquidity, making them suitable for swing trading strategies.

7. Timing Entry and Exit: Swing traders enter trades during a trend and exit when the trend changes or when their profit targets or stop-loss levels are reached. This requires careful monitoring of market conditions and the ability to make informed trading decisions based on technical and fundamental analysis.

Overall, swing trading is a strategy that can be potentially profitable in trending markets but requires patience, risk management, and a disciplined approach to trading.

| 6. POSITION TRADING

| Buy and sell over a period of months or years, holding positions for multiple months or years. | Can be profitable in long-term trends. | Requires a lot of patience, can be difficult to identify long-term trends. | 5-10% of account | 5-10 ATR | 5-10 ATR | Trending pairs, e.g., EUR/USD, GBP/USD | Long-term trends |

Position trading involves buying and selling financial instruments, typically currency pairs in forex, over an extended period, ranging from months to years. Traders who engage in position trading hold their positions for multiple months or even years, aiming to profit from long-term market trends.

While position trading can be potentially profitable, it requires a great deal of patience and discipline. Identifying long-term trends can be challenging, and traders need to have the ability to withstand market fluctuations and stay committed to their positions even during periods of drawdown.

In terms of risk management, position traders typically allocate a small portion of their account, around 5-10%, to each trade. They also use stop-loss orders to limit potential losses and take profit orders to lock in gains.

The average true range (ATR) is a technical indicator that measures market volatility. Position traders often use the ATR to determine appropriate stop-loss levels and to gauge potential profit targets.

Trending pairs, such as EUR/USD and GBP/USD, are commonly favored by position traders due to their tendency to exhibit strong and sustained trends.

Indeed, position trading is a long-term trading strategy that requires patience, discipline, and a deep understanding of market dynamics. It is suitable for traders who are willing to commit to trades for extended periods in pursuit of potentially significant profits from long-term trends.

| 7. CARRY TRADE

| Borrow money in a low-interest-rate currency and invest it in a high-interest-rate currency. | Can be profitable if the interest rate differential is large enough. | Currency risk, interest rate risk. | 1-2% of account | 2-3 ATR | 1-2 ATR | Pairs with a large interest rate differential, e.g., AUD/JPY, NZD/JPY | When the interest rate differential is large |

Borrowing money in a low-interest-rate currency and investing it in a high-interest-rate currency can be a profitable strategy if the interest rate differential is large enough. However, there are risks involved, including currency risk and interest rate risk. Please note: you can't use this strategy by buying and selling two pairs. You must use a broker who allows actual borrowing. Some traders claim profitable trading by shorting the low interest pair and long trade the high interest pair after weeks or months. Paper trade first and see what happens. You could find the fortune cookie.

Currency Risk:

Currency risk is the risk that the value of one currency will change relative to another currency. This means that the investment could lose value if the currency in which it is invested weakens against the currency in which the loan is denominated.

Interest Rate Risk:

Interest rate risk is the risk that interest rates will change, which could affect the profitability of the investment. If interest rates rise in the currency in which the loan is denominated, the cost of borrowing will increase, reducing the profit margin. Conversely, if interest rates fall in the currency in which the investment is made, the return on the investment will decrease.

Profitability:

The profitability of this strategy depends on the size of the interest rate differential and the costs involved in borrowing and investing the money.

Risks:

The main risks of this strategy are currency risk, interest rate risk, and the potential for losses if the investment does not perform as expected.

Suitable Conditions:

This strategy is most suitable when the interest rate differential is large and the risks are manageable.

Examples:

A common example of this strategy is to borrow money in Japanese Yen (JPY) and invest it in Australian Dollars (AUD). The interest rate differential between these two currencies is often large, and the risks are relatively low.

How can you do that trading the Forex? To trade the Forex using the carry trade strategy, you can follow these steps:

1. Choose a Currency Pair with a Large Interest Rate Differential:

Look for currency pairs where the interest rate differential is large and stable. This means that the interest rate in the currency you are borrowing should be significantly lower than the interest rate in the currency you are investing in.

2. Open a Forex Trading Account:

Once you have chosen a currency pair, you need to open a Forex trading account with a reputable broker.

3. Borrow Money in the Low-Interest-Rate Currency:

Use your trading account to borrow money in the currency with the lower interest rate. This is called the "funding currency."

4. Invest the Borrowed Money in the High-Interest-Rate Currency:

Use the borrowed money to buy the currency with the higher interest rate. This is called the "target currency."

5. Hold the Position:

Hold the position for a period of time, typically several weeks or months. During this time, you will earn interest on the borrowed money and the invested money.

6. Close the Position:

When you are ready to close the position, sell the target currency and use the proceeds to repay the loan.

7. Profit or Loss:

If the interest rate differential is large enough, you will make a profit on the trade. However, if the interest rate differential narrows or if the value of the target currency falls against the funding currency, you could lose money.

It is important to note that the carry trade strategy is a leveraged trading strategy, which means that it can magnify both profits and losses. Therefore, it is important to manage your risk carefully and to use stop-loss orders to protect your capital.

When you say borrow, do you mean short trade? Borrowing in Forex trading does not directly translate to a short trade. In a short trade, a trader sells a currency pair, expecting its value to decrease. This means the trader is selling the base currency and buying the quote currency.

In a carry trade, borrowing refers to obtaining funds in a currency with a low-interest rate. This is done by entering into a currency forward contract, where the trader agrees to exchange one currency for another at a specific exchange rate on a future date. The trader is essentially borrowing the funding currency at the current exchange rate and committing to repay it at the future exchange rate.

The borrowed funds are then used to buy a currency with a higher interest rate. The trader holds this position for a period of time, earning interest on the borrowed funds and the invested funds. If the interest rate differential is large enough and the exchange rate between the two currencies remains stable or moves in the trader's favor, the trader can profit from the carry trade.

Therefore, while a carry trade involves borrowing funds, it does not directly correspond to a short trade in Forex. In a carry trade, the trader is entering into a forward contract to borrow one currency and invest it in another currency, whereas in a short trade, the trader is selling a currency pair, expecting its value to decrease.

| 8. HEDGING

| Take opposite positions in two or more correlated assets. | Can be used to reduce risk. | Can be expensive, can be difficult to manage multiple positions. | 1-2% of account | 1-2 ATR | 1-2 ATR | Correlated pairs, e.g., EUR/USD, GBP/USD | When correlation is high |

Hedging is a strategy that involves taking opposite positions in two or more correlated assets. Its primary purpose is to reduce risk by offsetting the potential losses from one asset with the potential gains from another. Here is a breakdown of the key points:

1. Risk Reduction: Hedging is primarily used to reduce the risk of an investment portfolio. By creating a correlation between two assets, investors can balance the upswings and downswings, reducing the overall risk exposure.

2. Expense and Complexity: While hedging can be an effective risk management tool, it can also be expensive and complex. The cost of setting up and maintaining multiple positions can be substantial. Additionally, managing multiple positions can be challenging, especially for inexperienced investors.

3. Allocation: Hedging typically involves allocating a small portion of an investment portfolio, typically around 1-2% of the total account value. This allocation is intended to balance risk without sacrificing potential returns from other investments.

4. ATR (Average True Range): Hedging parameters often

incorporate the Average True Range (ATR), a measure of volatility. The ATR is used to set stop-loss levels and position sizing for the hedging strategy.

5. Correlated Pairs: Hedging is commonly applied to correlated pairs of assets, such as EUR/USD and GBP/USD. Correlated pairs move in the same direction, allowing investors to hedge one position with the other.

6. High Correlation 80+: The effectiveness of hedging depends on the correlation between the assets. When the correlation is high, the hedging strategy is more likely to achieve its goal of reducing risk.

| 9. OPTIONS TRADING

| Buy or sell options on a currency pair. | Can be used to speculate or hedge. | Options can be complex and risky. | 1-2% of account | 2-3 ATR | 1-2 ATR | Liquid pairs, e.g., EUR/USD, GBP/USD | When volatility is high |

Strategy: Buy or sell options on a currency pair.

Purpose: Options trading can be used for speculation or hedging.

Complexity and Risk: Options can be complex and risky financial instruments. It is important to understand the risks involved before trading options.

Recommended Allocation: Allocate a small portion of your trading account to options trading, typically around 1-2%.

Recommended Risk Parameters: Use stop-loss orders to manage risk. The stop-loss level should be set at a distance of 2-3 times the average true range (ATR) for the currency pair being traded. The profit target should be set at a distance of 1-2 times the ATR.

Suitable Market Conditions: Options trading is best suited for liquid currency pairs, such as EUR/USD, GBP/USD, etc. It is also more effective when market volatility is high.

| 10. FOREX ROBOTS

| Use a computer program to automate trading. | Can be profitable if used correctly. | Can be expensive, can be difficult to set up and manage. | 1-2% of account | 2-3 ATR | 1-2 ATR | Any pair 24/5 |

Tactic: Using a computer program to automate trading decisions. See section 38 for a working model.

Strategy: Forex robots are computer programs that are designed to automatically execute trades in the foreign exchange market. They can be programmed to use a variety of trading strategies, such as technical analysis, fundamental analysis, or a combination of both.

Pros:

Forex robots can trade 24/5, which means that they can take advantage of market opportunities even when traders are not available.

Forex robots can be profitable if they are used correctly. They can help traders to identify and execute trades that they would not be able to find on their own.

Forex robots can help traders to avoid making emotional trading decisions.

Cons:

Forex robots can be expensive to purchase and maintain.

Forex robots can be difficult to set up and manage.

Forex robots can be risky if they are not used correctly. They can lead to losses if they are not programmed properly or if they are not monitored closely.

Position Sizing: 1-2% of account

Stop Loss: 2-3 ATR

Take Profit: 1-2 ATR

Appropriate Pair: Any pair

Timing: 24/5

| 11. MOVING AVERAGES

| Use moving averages to identify trends and reversals. | Easy to understand, can be profitable in trending markets. | Can be difficult to identify trends in choppy markets, can be whipsawed in volatile markets. | 1-2% of account | 2-3 ATR | 1-2 ATR | Trending pairs, e.g., EUR/USD, GBP/USD | Follow the trend |

The Behemoth

Moving averages are technical indicators that help traders identify trends and reversals in the market. They are easy to understand and can be profitable in trending markets. However, moving averages can be difficult to identify in choppy markets and can lead to whipsawing in volatile markets.

Recommendations:

- Risk: Allocate 1-2% of your trading account to each trade using a moving average strategy.

- Stop Loss: Place a stop loss order 2-3 times the ATR (Average True Range) away from your entry point.

- Take Profit: Take profit when the price reaches 1-2 ATRs away from your entry point.

- Best Markets: Moving average strategies work best in trending pairs, such as EUR/USD and GBP/USD.

- Trading Plan: Follow the trend identified by the moving average.

The most common moving averages in specific time frames:

- Short-term moving averages: 5, 10, and 15 periods are used to identify short-term trends and reversals.

- Medium-term moving averages: 20, 50, and 100 periods are used to identify medium-term trends and reversals.

- Long-term moving averages: 200 and 400 periods are used to identify long-term trends and reversals.

Traders can use different combinations of moving averages to create trading strategies that suit their risk tolerance and trading style.

| 12. SUPPORT AND RESISTANCE

| Buy near support levels, sell near resistance levels. | Easy to understand, can be profitable in ranging markets. | Can be difficult to identify support and resistance levels, can be broken in volatile markets. | 1-2% of account | 2-3 ATR | 1-2 ATR | Range-bound pairs, e.g., EUR/JPY, GBP/JPY | Near support/resistance levels |

1. Strategy: Support and Resistance Trading

2. Key Points:

- Buy near support levels: When the price of a currency pair declines to a level where it has historically bounced back, it is a potential buying opportunity. This is because there is a higher probability that the price will rebound from this level rather than continue to decline.

- Sell near resistance levels: When the price of a currency pair rises to a level where it has historically stalled or reversed, it is a potential selling opportunity. This is because there is a higher probability that the price will either stall or reverse from this level rather than continue to climb.

- Easy to understand and potentially profitable: The concept of support and resistance is relatively easy to understand, making it a popular strategy for both novice and experienced traders.

Additionally, it can be a profitable strategy, especially in ranging markets where the price of a currency pair fluctuates within a specific range.

- Challenges:

- Identifying support and resistance levels: Accurately identifying support and resistance levels can be challenging, especially for novice traders. This is because these levels are not always clearly defined and can change over time.

- Volatile markets: Support and resistance levels can be broken in volatile markets, which can lead to losses for traders who have placed trades based on these levels.

3. Risk Management:

- Risk per trade: Traders should aim to risk 1-2% of their trading account on each trade. This will help to limit their losses in the event that a trade goes against them.

- Stop-loss placement: Traders should place a stop-loss order a few pips below the support level (for long trades) or a few pips above the resistance level (for short trades). This will help to limit their losses in the event that the support or resistance level is broken.

- Take-profit placement: Traders should set a take-profit target that is 2-3 times the size of their stop-loss. This will help to ensure that they are taking profits when the market moves in their favor.

4. Recommended Markets:

- Range-bound pairs: Support and resistance trading is best suited for range-bound currency pairs, such as EUR/JPY and GBP/JPY. These pairs tend to fluctuate within a specific range, making it easier to identify support and resistance levels.

5. Entry and Exit Points:

- Entry: Traders should enter trades near support or resistance levels, depending on whether they are taking a long or short position.

- Exit: Traders should exit trades when the price reaches their take-profit target or when the support or resistance level is broken.

| 13. BOLLINGER BANDS

| Use Bollinger Bands to identify overbought/oversold conditions. | Easy to understand, can be profitable in mean-reverting markets. | Can be difficult to identify overbought/oversold conditions, can be whipsawed in volatile markets. | 1% of account | 1-2 ATR | 1-2 ATR | Range-bound pairs, e.g., EUR/JPY, GBP/JPY | Oversold/overbought conditions |

Bollinger Bands can help traders identify potential overbought or oversold conditions in the market. This can be useful for determining when to buy or sell a currency pair. However, it's important to note that Bollinger Bands are not foolproof, and they can sometimes give false signals. Therefore, it's important to use them in conjunction with other trading indicators to confirm the signals.

One potential advantage of using Bollinger Bands is that they are relatively simple to understand. Even beginner traders can quickly learn how to use them. Additionally, Bollinger Bands can be profitable in mean-reverting markets, where prices tend to oscillate between a range of values.

However, there are also some potential disadvantages associated with using Bollinger Bands. One disadvantage is that it can be difficult to accurately identify overbought or oversold conditions in the market. This can lead to false signals, which can result in losses. Another disadvantage is that Bollinger

Bands can be whipsawed in volatile markets. This means that prices can move quickly outside of the Bollinger Bands, which can lead to unnecessary trades and losses.

Overall, Bollinger Bands can be a useful tool for traders, but it's important to use them correctly. Traders should be aware of the potential advantages and disadvantages of Bollinger Bands before using them in their trading.

Example:

Let's say that you are trading the EUR/JPY currency pair. You notice that the price has been trading within a range for several weeks. You decide to use Bollinger Bands to help you identify potential trading opportunities.

You set the Bollinger Bands to 2 standard deviations above and below the moving average. You notice that the price has recently crossed below the lower Bollinger Band. This indicates that the EUR/JPY currency pair is oversold and may be due for a bounce.

You decide to place a long trade, with a stop loss below the lower Bollinger Band and a take profit target above the upper Bollinger Band. If the trade is successful, you will make a profit. However, if the trade is unsuccessful, you will lose money.

| 14. ICHIMOKU KINKO HYO

| Use Ichimoku Kinko Hyo to identify trends, turning points, and support and resistance levels. | Comprehensive trading system, can be profitable in trending and ranging markets. | Can be complex to learn, can be difficult to interpret signals. | 1-2% of account | 2-3 ATR | 1-2 ATR | Any pair | 24/5 |

Ichimoku Kinko Hyo, a versatile trading system, offers insights into market trends, turning points, and support or resistance levels. Despite its complexity, mastering its signals yields substantial rewards. It's recommended to risk 1-2% of your account, placing a stop-loss 2-3 ATR (Average True Range) away from the entry price and taking profit at 1-2 ATR. This strategy applies to any currency pair and can be traded around the clock. Please read the section after the glossary.

| 15. PRICE ACTION TRADING

| Trade based on price action, without using indicators. | Can be profitable in trending and ranging markets. | Requires experience and skill, can be difficult to identify trading opportunities. | 1% of account | 1-2 ATR | 1-2 ATR | Any pair | 24/5 |

Description: This strategy involves trading based solely on the price action of a financial instrument, without using any technical indicators. It relies on the trader's ability to identify patterns and trends in the price movements to make trading decisions.

Profitability: This strategy can be profitable in both trending and ranging markets. However, it requires considerable experience and skill to identify trading opportunities accurately.

Risk: The recommended risk per trade is 1% of the account balance.

Stop Loss and Take Profit: The recommended stop loss and take profit levels are 1-2 Average True Range (ATR) for both.

Suitable Currency Pairs: This strategy can be applied to any currency pair.

Recommended Trading Frequency: This strategy is best suited for intraday trading, with a recommended trading frequency of 24 trades per week.

| 16. BREAKOUT TRADING

| Buy when the price breaks above a resistance level, sell when it breaks below a support level. | Can be profitable in trending markets. | Can be difficult to identify false breakouts, can be whipsawed in choppy markets. | 1-2% of account | 2-3 ATR | 1-2 ATR | Trending pairs, e.g., EUR/USD, GBP/USD | Breakouts |

Breakout Trading is a strategy that involves buying when the price breaks above a resistance level and selling when it breaks below a support level. This strategy can be profitable in trending markets, where the price is moving consistently in one direction. However, breakout trading can also be difficult, as it can be challenging to identify false breakouts and traders can be whipsawed in choppy markets.

To trade breakouts effectively, traders typically use a risk-to-reward ratio of 1:2 or 1:3, meaning that they risk 1 unit of currency for the potential to make 2 or 3 units of currency. They also typically set their stop loss at 1-2 ATR (Average True Range) below the entry price for long positions and 1-2 ATR above the entry price for short positions.

Breakout trading is best suited for trending currency pairs, such as EUR/USD and GBP/USD. Traders should look for breakouts that occur in the direction of the trend, as these are more likely to be successful.

| 17. PULLBACK TRADING

| Buy when the price pulls back to a support level, sell when it pulls back to a resistance level. | Can be profitable in trending markets. | Can be difficult to identify false pullbacks, can be whipsawed in choppy markets. | 1-2% of account | 2-3 ATR | 1-2 ATR | Trending pairs, e.g., EUR/USD, GBP/USD | Pullbacks |

Pullback trading is a trading strategy that involves buying when the price of an asset pulls back to a support level, and selling when it pulls back to a resistance level. This strategy can be profitable in trending markets, as it allows traders to enter trades at favorable prices. However, it can be difficult to identify false pullbacks, which can lead to whipsawed trades in choppy markets.

To implement this strategy, traders should look for assets that are trending strongly. Once a trend has been identified, traders can use technical analysis to identify support and resistance levels. When the price of an asset pulls back to a support level, traders can buy the asset, with the expectation that it will continue to trend higher. When the price of an asset pulls back to a resistance level, traders can sell the asset, with the expectation that it will continue to trend lower.

The risk-to-reward ratio for pullback trading is typically favorable, as traders can enter trades at prices that are below the current market price. However, it is important to note that there is a risk of false pullbacks, which can lead to losing trades. Therefore, it is important to use sound risk management techniques, such as stop-loss orders, to protect your trading account.

Indeed pullback trading can be a profitable trading strategy, but it is important to understand the risks involved and to use sound risk management techniques.

| 18. REVERSAL TRADING

| Buy when the price reverses from a downtrend to an uptrend, sell when it reverses from an uptrend to a downtrend. | Can be profitable in trending markets. | Can be difficult to identify reversals, can be whipsawed in choppy markets. | 1-2% of account | 2-3 ATR | 1-2 ATR | Trending pairs, e.g., EUR/USD, GBP/USD | Reversals |

Interpretation

1. Strategy: Reversal Trading

   - Buy when the price reverses from a downtrend to an uptrend.

   - Sell when the price reverses from an uptrend to a downtrend.

2. Market Conditions:

   - Can be profitable in trending markets.

3. Challenges:

   - Can be difficult to identify reversals.

   - Can be whipsawed in choppy markets.

4. Risk Management:

- Risk 1-2% of the trading account per trade.

5. Position Sizing:

- Use 2-3 times the Average True Range (ATR) as the initial stop loss.

6. Profit Target:

- Target 1-2 times the ATR for each trade.

7. Suitable Markets:

- Trending currency pairs, such as EUR/USD and GBP/USD.

8. Trading Signal:

- Reversals

Indeed, reversal trading involves buying when the price reverses from a downtrend to an uptrend and selling when it reverses from an uptrend to a downtrend. This strategy can be profitable in trending markets, but it can be challenging to identify reversals and traders can be whipsawed in choppy markets. It's important to use proper risk management techniques, such as limiting risk to a small percentage of the trading account and using appropriate position sizing and stop loss levels.

| 19. TREND CONTINUATION TRADING

| Buy when the price continues an uptrend, sell when it continues a downtrend. | Can be profitable in trending markets. | Can be difficult to identify trend continuations, can be whipsawed in choppy markets. | 1-2% of account | 2-3 ATR | 1-2 ATR | Trending pairs, e.g., EUR/USD, GBP/USD | Trend continuations |

1. Trading Strategy: Trend continuation trading involves buying when the price continues an uptrend and selling when it continues a downtrend.

2. Profitability: This strategy can be profitable in trending markets, where prices are consistently moving in one direction.

3. Challenges: Identifying trend continuations can be challenging. Additionally, whipsawing can occur in choppy markets, leading to losing trades.

4. Risk Management: It is recommended to risk 1-2% of the trading account per trade.

5. Stop Loss: A stop loss should be placed 2-3 ATR (Average True Range) away from the entry price to limit potential losses.

6. Take Profit: A take profit target should be set 1-2 ATR away from the entry price to secure profits.

7. Suitable Markets: Trend continuation trading is best suited for trending pairs, such as EUR/USD and GBP/USD.

8. Trading Conditions: This strategy is most effective when there is a clear trend in the market and not during choppy or range-bound conditions.

| 20. RANGE TRADING

| Buy near the bottom of a range, sell near the top of a range. | Can be profitable in range-bound markets. | Can be difficult to identify ranges, can be whipsawed in trending markets. | 1-2% of account | 2-3 ATR | 1-2 ATR | Range-bound pairs, e.g., EUR/JPY, GBP/JPY | Ranges | Tactic | Strategy | Pros | Cons | Position Sizing | Stop Loss | Take Profit | Appropriate Pair | Timing |

Range trading is a trading strategy that involves buying near the bottom of a price range and selling near the top of the range. This strategy can be profitable in range-bound markets, where the price of an asset fluctuates within a defined range.

Pros of Range Trading:

Can be profitable in range-bound markets.

Relatively low risk, as the trader is not trying to predict the direction of the market.

Can be used with a variety of financial instruments, including stocks, commodities, and currencies.

Cons of Range Trading:

Can be difficult to identify ranges, as the price of an asset can break out of a range at any time.

Can be whipsawed in trending markets, where the price of an asset moves consistently in one direction.

Appropriate Pair for Range Trading:

Range-bound pairs, such as EUR/JPY and GBP/JPY.

Timing for Range Trading:

Ranges are typically identified using technical analysis, such as support and resistance levels.

Position Sizing for Range Trading:

1-2% of account.

Stop Loss for Range Trading:

2-3 ATR (Average True Range).

Take Profit for Range Trading:

1-2 ATR (Average True Range).

| 21. MOMENTUM TRADING

| Buy when the price is rising quickly, sell when it is falling quickly. | Can be profitable in trending markets. | Can be difficult to identify momentum reversals, can be whipsawed in choppy markets. | 1-2% of account | 2-3 ATR | 1-2 ATR | Trending pairs, e.g., EUR/USD, GBP/USD | During strong trends |

Concept:
Identify and trade in the direction of strong market trends, buying when prices are rising quickly and selling when they are falling quickly.

Profitability:
Momentum trading can be profitable, particularly in trending markets where prices exhibit clear directional movements.

Challenges:
The primary challenges in momentum trading are:

1. Identifying Momentum Reversals: Determining when a trend is reversing direction can be difficult, leading to potential losses if trades are not exited at the right time.

2. Whipsawing in Choppy Markets: Momentum strategies can be vulnerable to whipsawing, a situation where prices move erratically in both directions, resulting in frequent losing trades.

Risk Management:

Appropriate risk management is crucial in momentum trading, with specific considerations including:

1. Position Size: Limiting the size of each trade relative to the overall account balance helps to mitigate potential losses.

2. Stop Loss Placement: Using stoploss orders to automatically exit trades when prices move against the trader's position helps to limit losses.

3. ATR: The Average True Range (ATR) is a volatility measure that can help determine appropriate stoploss levels and position sizes.

Suitable Market Conditions:
Momentum trading is most effective in trending markets with strong directional price movements. It is less suitable for choppy or sideways markets.

Recommended Trading Pairs:
Trending currency pairs such as EUR/USD and GBP/USD are typically preferred for momentum trading strategies.

Trade Execution:
Momentum trades are typically executed during periods of strong price movement, such as during news events or market rallies.

| 22. NEWS TRADING

| Trade based on news events. | Can be profitable if you can get the news before the market does. | News events can be difficult to predict, can be whipsawed by false news. | 1-2% of account | 2-3 ATR | 1-2 ATR | Any pair | News events |

Concept:

News trading involves making trades based on significant news events that can impact the financial markets.

Potential for Profit:

News trading can be potentially profitable if traders can access and interpret news events before they are reflected in market prices. By doing so, traders may be able to capitalize on market movements that result from the news.

Challenges:

News events can be challenging to predict accurately. There is always the risk of whipsawing, where the market moves in the opposite direction of the anticipated move, due to false news or unexpected developments.

Risk Management:

To manage risk in news trading, traders should consider the following:

Allocating a small portion (12%) of their trading account to news trades.

Setting stoploss orders at an appropriate distance from the entry price (23 ATRs).

Taking profit targets at a reasonable level (12 ATRs).

Preferred Currency Pairs:

News trading can be applied to any currency pair, as significant news events can affect all financial markets.

Timing:

News trading typically focuses on trading around news events that are scheduled in advance, such as economic data releases, central bank meetings, and political developments.

| 23. CORRELATION TRADING

| Trade two or more correlated pairs in the same direction. | Can be profitable if the correlation is strong. | Correlation can change, can be whipsawed if the correlation breaks down. | 1-2% of account | 2-3 ATR | 1-2 ATR | Correlated pairs, e.g., EUR/USD, GBP/USD | When correlation is high |

A common mistake is to think that USD/CHF is correlated to EUR/USD: think twice. This alone is worth several times the price of this work.

Correlation trading is a strategy that involves trading two or more correlated pairs in the same direction. This strategy can be profitable if the correlation between the pairs is strong, as it increases the likelihood that both pairs will move in the same direction.

Key Points

1. Identify Correlated Pairs:

Identify pairs of instruments that exhibit a strong correlation in their price movements. These pairs typically move in the same direction, increasing the likelihood of a profitable trade.

2. Choose a Trading Direction:

Once correlated pairs are identified, choose a trading direction based on technical analysis or fundamental research. If the correlation between the pairs is positive and both instruments are trending upwards, a long position can be considered. Conversely, if the correlation is negative and both instruments are trending downwards, a short position may be suitable.

3. Manage Risk:

Correlation trading involves trading multiple pairs simultaneously, which can potentially increase risk. Manage risk by diversifying the portfolio, setting appropriate stop-loss orders, and maintaining a reasonable leverage level.

4. Be Prepared for Correlation Breakdowns:

Correlations between pairs can change over time. If the correlation between the pairs changes or breaks down, it can lead to losses. Be prepared for these potential changes by monitoring the correlation and adjusting trading strategies accordingly.

Example

Consider the correlated pair of EUR/USD and GBP/USD. If both pairs are trending upwards and have a strong positive correlation, a trader might consider buying both pairs. If the correlation remains strong and both pairs continue to trend upwards, the trader could potentially profit from both trades.

Risks and Considerations

Correlation Breakdown: Correlations can change over time, and if the correlation between the pairs breaks down, it can lead to losses.

Increased Risk: Trading multiple pairs simultaneously can potentially increase risk. Proper risk management techniques need to be employed.

Difficulty in Identifying Correlated Pairs: Identifying pairs with a strong and consistent correlation can be challenging.

False Signals: Correlation trading relies on the assumption that correlated pairs will continue moving in the same direction. However, this assumption is not always accurate, and false signals can occur, leading to losses.

| 24. TREND FOLLOWING WITH MULTIPLE TIMEFRAMES

| Use multiple timeframes to identify the overall trend and then trade in the direction of that trend on a shorter timeframe. | Can be profitable in trending markets. | Can be difficult to identify the overall trend, can be whipsawed in choppy markets. | 1-2% of account | 2-3 ATR | 1-2 ATR | Trending pairs, e.g., EUR/USD, GBP/USD | Follow the trend |

Trend following with multiple timeframes is a trading strategy that involves analyzing the market on multiple timeframes to identify the overall trend and then trading in the direction of that trend on a shorter timeframe.

1. Choose Trending Pairs:

   - Select currency pairs that are known for trending behavior, such as EUR/USD, GBP/USD, or AUD/USD.

2. Analyze Multiple Timeframes:

   - Look at different timeframes, such as the daily, 4-hour, and 1-hour charts.

   - Identify the overall trend on the higher timeframes (e.g., daily).

- Use the shorter timeframes (e.g., 1-hour) to find trading opportunities in the direction of the overall trend.

3. Confirm Trend Direction:

- Use technical indicators like moving averages or trend lines to confirm the trend direction on each timeframe.

- Ensure that the trend is well-established and has some momentum behind it.

4. Enter Trades:

- Place trades in the direction of the overall trend on the shorter timeframe.

- Use limit or market orders to enter trades at favorable prices.

- Consider using a trailing stop loss to protect your profits.

5. Manage Risk:

- Define your risk tolerance and set appropriate position sizes.

- Use a risk management strategy, such as a stop loss or risk-reward ratio, to limit your potential losses.

6. Take Profits:

- Set realistic profit targets based on the identified trend and your risk-reward strategy.

- Close trades when your profit target is reached or if the trend reverses.

7. Monitor and Adjust:

- Continuously monitor the market and adjust your trading strategy as needed.

- Pay attention to changes in the overall trend or market conditions.

- Be prepared to exit trades early if the trend weakens or reverses.

This strategy can be profitable in trending markets, but it requires careful analysis and risk management. The key is to identify the overall trend accurately and to trade in line with that trend on a shorter timeframe. It is also important to be aware of the potential risks, such as whipsaws and false signals, and to adjust your strategy accordingly.

| 25. FIBONACCI TRADING

| Use Fibonacci retracement levels to identify potential support and resistance levels. | Can be profitable in ranging markets. | Fibonacci levels can be subjective, can be broken in volatile markets. | 1-2% of account | 2-3 ATR | 1-2 ATR | Range-bound pairs, e.g., EUR/JPY, GBP/JPY | Near Fibonacci levels |

Fibonacci trading is a technical analysis strategy that utilizes the Fibonacci sequence to identify potential areas of support and resistance in financial markets. These levels are determined by applying Fibonacci ratios to the price action of a security. Traders then use these levels to make informed decisions about potential trading opportunities.

Key Points

1. Fibonacci Retracement Levels:

- Fibonacci retracement levels are drawn using the Fibonacci sequence (0, 1, 1, 2, 3, 5, 8, 13, 21, 34, etc.).

- These levels represent potential retracement areas after a significant price move.

2. Identifying Support and Resistance:

- Fibonacci retracement levels are often used to identify potential support and resistance levels.

- Support levels are areas where a downtrend is expected to pause or reverse.

- Resistance levels are areas where an uptrend is expected to pause or reverse.

3. Profitability in Ranging Markets:

- Fibonacci trading can be profitable in ranging markets, where prices fluctuate within a defined range.

- During these periods, Fibonacci retracement levels can be used to identify potential turning points and trade accordingly.

4. Subjectivity and Volatility:

- Fibonacci levels are subjective and can be interpreted differently by different traders.

- In volatile markets, Fibonacci levels can be broken easily, making them less reliable for trading.

5. Risk Management:

- As with any trading strategy, risk management is crucial in Fibonacci trading.

- It is advisable to risk only 1-2% of your trading account balance on each trade.

6. Stop-Loss and Take-Profit:

- Place a stop-loss order below the support level (for long trades) or above the resistance level (for short trades) to limit your risk.

- Set your take-profit target at a Fibonacci retracement level that offers a favorable risk-to-reward ratio.

7. Suitable Markets:

- Fibonacci trading is often applied to range-bound currency pairs, such as EUR/JPY and GBP/JPY.

- These pairs tend to exhibit recurring patterns and retracements, making them suitable for this strategy.

8. Trade Entry and Exit:

- Look for trading opportunities near Fibonacci retracement levels.

- Enter a long trade when the price bounces off a support level and vice versa for short trades.

- Exit your trade when the price reaches your predetermined take-profit level or stop-loss level.

Conclusion:

Fibonacci trading is a technical analysis strategy that utilizes Fibonacci retracement levels to identify potential trading opportunities. While it can be profitable in ranging markets, it is important to note that Fibonacci levels are subjective and can be broken in volatile markets. As with any trading strategy, risk management and careful trade execution are essential for success.

Ah, how to really trade with Fibonacci levels

1. Identify Key Fibonacci Levels:

   - 0.00 (Start of Fibonacci sequence)

   - 0.236 (23.6% retracement level)

   - 0.382 (38.2% retracement level)

- 0.500 (50% retracement level)

- 0.618 (61.8% retracement level)

- 0.786 (78.6% retracement level)

- 1.00 (100% retracement level)

Note: the levels are automatically drawn by advanced charts.

2. Plot Fibonacci Levels on Chart:

- Use a trading platform or technical analysis software that allows you to plot Fibonacci levels.

- Draw Fibonacci lines from a significant high to a significant low (or vice versa) on the chart.

3. Identify Potential Trading Opportunities:

- Look for price action that interacts with Fibonacci levels in the following ways:

- Support: Price may bounce off a Fibonacci support level (e.g., 0.382 or 0.618) and resume an uptrend.

- Resistance: Price may face resistance at a Fibonacci resistance level (e.g., 0.236 or 0.786) and begin a downtrend.

- Breakouts: Price may break through a Fibonacci level with momentum, indicating a potential continuation of the trend.

4. Place Market Orders or Set Pending Orders:

- Based on your analysis, determine appropriate entry and exit points for trades.

- Consider using limit orders to enter trades at specific prices near Fibonacci levels.

- Place stop-loss orders below support levels or above resistance levels to manage risk.

5. Manage Your Risk:

- Always use appropriate risk management strategies, such as setting stop-loss orders, using position sizing, and managing overall portfolio risk.

- Remember that Fibonacci levels are not a guarantee of future price movements and should be used in conjunction with other technical indicators and analysis.

6. Back test and Monitor Trades:

- Test your Fibonacci trading strategy on historical data to assess its effectiveness.

- Continuously monitor your trades and adjust as needed, considering market conditions and changes in price action.

| 26. ELLIOTT WAVE TRADING

| Use Elliott wave theory to identify potential turning points in the market. | Can be profitable in trending markets. | Elliott wave theory can be complex, can be difficult to interpret signals. | 1-2% of account | 2-3 ATR | 1-2 ATR | Any pair | Turning points |

1. Identify the Trend:

- Determine the current market trend (uptrend, downtrend, or sideways).

- Elliott wave theory suggests that markets move in waves, and identifying the trend helps determine the direction of the next wave.

2. Recognize Wave Patterns:

- Study the Elliott wave patterns, which consist of impulsive waves (1-5) and corrective waves (A-B-C).

- Impulsive waves move in the direction of the trend, while corrective waves move against the trend.

3. Identify Elliott Wave Levels:

- Elliott wave theory divides the market into Fibonacci levels (such as 38.2%, 50%, and 61.8%).

- These levels often act as support and resistance levels, and traders look for price action signals near these levels.

4. Confirm Signals:

- Use technical indicators, such as moving averages, oscillators, and support and resistance levels, to confirm Elliott wave signals.

- Wait for multiple indicators to align before taking a trade, as this increases the probability of a successful trade.

5. Enter and Manage Trades:

- Enter a trade in the direction of the identified wave.

- Set stop-loss orders below the entry point for long trades and above the entry point for short trades to limit risk.

- Manage trades based on Elliott wave theory principles, such as wave extensions and retracements, to adjust position size and targets.

6. Trade Management:

- Continuously monitor the market and adjust your trading strategy as needed.

- Be prepared to close trades early if the market conditions change or if the Elliott wave pattern breaks down.

- Manage risk effectively by controlling position size and using appropriate leverage.

| 27. VOLUME TRADING

| Trade based on volume. | Can be profitable in trending and ranging markets. | Volume can be misleading, can be difficult to interpret signals. | 1-2% of account | 2-3 ATR | 1-2 ATR | Any pair | High volume periods |

Volume Trading: Volume trading is a trading strategy that involves buying or selling a financial instrument based on the volume of trading activity. The idea is that high volume can indicate a strong trend or a potential reversal, and that trading in the direction of the volume can be profitable.

Volume in Trending and Ranging Markets: Volume trading can be profitable in both trending and ranging markets. In trending markets, high volume can confirm the trend and provide opportunities to enter or exit trades. In ranging markets, high volume can indicate a potential breakout or reversal.

Volume Interpretation: Volume can be misleading, and it can be difficult to interpret the signals it provides. For example, high volume can sometimes indicate a strong trend, but it can also indicate a market that is topping out or bottoming out. It is important to consider other factors, such as price action, moving averages, and support and resistance levels, when making trading decisions based on volume.

Risk Management: When trading based on volume, it is important to manage risk carefully. This includes using stop-loss orders to limit potential losses, and trading with a small position size relative to your account size.

Suitable Currency Pairs: Volume trading can be applied to any currency pair. However, some pairs are more liquid and have higher trading volumes than others. These pairs are generally easier to trade and provide more opportunities for profitable trades.

Best Trading Times: The best times to trade based on volume are during periods of high volume. This is typically during the London and New York trading sessions. However, there can also be periods of high volume during the Asian trading session.

| 28. SEASONALITY TRADING

| Trade based on seasonal patterns. | Can be profitable in seasonal markets. | Seasonal patterns can change, can be difficult to identify reliable patterns. | 1-2% of account | 2-3 ATR | 1-2 ATR | Seasonal pairs, e.g., EUR/USD, GBP/USD | Seasonal periods |

Summary:

- Seasonality Trading involves identifying and trading based on recurring seasonal patterns in the market.

- This strategy can be potentially profitable in markets that exhibit strong seasonal trends.

- However, seasonal patterns are subject to change and can be difficult to identify with certainty.

Key Points

1. Account Allocation:

   - Allocate 1-2% of your trading account to this strategy.

2. Stop Loss:

   - Set a stop loss of 2-3 times the Average True Range (ATR) to manage risk.

3. Take Profit:

- Take profits at a target level of 1-2 times the ATR to secure gains.

4. Suitable Markets:

- Seasonal trading is suitable for currency pairs that exhibit strong seasonal patterns, such as EUR/USD and GBP/USD.

5. Seasonal Periods:

- Identify seasonal periods and trade during these periods when the patterns are most likely to occur.

| 29. SENTIMENT TRADING

| Trade based on market sentiment. | Can be profitable if you can accurately gauge market sentiment. | Market sentiment can be difficult to measure, can be whipsawed by sudden changes in sentiment. | 1-2% of account | 2-3 ATR | 1-2 ATR | Any pair | Periods of strong sentiment |

Sentiment trading involves basing trading decisions on the prevailing market sentiment. This means attempting to gauge the overall attitude of market participants, whether they are bullish (optimistic) or bearish (pessimistic), and then trading accordingly.

Advantages:

1. Potential for Profitability: If you can accurately gauge market sentiment, sentiment trading can be profitable. When market sentiment is strongly bullish, you can buy with the expectation that prices will continue to rise. Conversely, when market sentiment is strongly bearish, you can sell with the expectation that prices will fall.

2. Widely Applicable: Sentiment trading can be applied to any financial market, including forex, stocks, commodities, and indices.

3. Short-Term Trading: Sentiment trading is often used for short-term trading, as market sentiment can change rapidly.

Disadvantages:

1. Difficulty in Measuring Market Sentiment: Market sentiment can be challenging to measure accurately. There are various indicators and techniques that traders use to gauge sentiment, but there is no single foolproof method.

2. Whipsawing: Sentiment can be subject to sudden changes, leading to whipsawing, where prices move in one direction and then reverse quickly, causing traders to lose money on both sides of the trade.

3. High Risk: Sentiment trading can be risky, especially if market sentiment changes unexpectedly. This can lead to significant losses if traders are not careful.

Risk Management:

1. Account Size: Traders should risk no more than 1-2% of their account on any single trade.

2. Stop Loss Orders: Traders should always use stop loss orders to limit their risk in case the market moves against them.

3. Position Sizing: Traders should adjust their position size based on their risk tolerance and the volatility of the market.

Trading Parameters:

1. Time Frame: Sentiment trading can be applied to any time

frame, but it is often used for short-term trading, such as intraday trading or swing trading.

2. Pairs: Sentiment trading can be applied to any currency pair.

3. Market Conditions: Sentiment trading is most effective during periods of strong market sentiment, which can occur during news events, economic data releases, or periods of high volatility.

| 30. PATTERN TRADING

| Trade based on chart patterns. | Can be profitable if you can accurately identify chart patterns. | Chart patterns can be subjective, can be broken in volatile markets. | 1-2% of account | 2-3 ATR | 1-2 ATR | Any pair | When chart patterns are forming | Tactic | Strategy | Pros | Cons | Position Sizing | Stop Loss | Take Profit | Appropriate Pair | Timing |

This strategy focuses on identifying and trading chart patterns in the forex market.

Pros:

1. Profitable with Accurate Pattern Identification: If traders can accurately identify chart patterns, this strategy has the potential to be profitable.

2. Simplicity: Pattern trading is relatively straightforward and easy to understand.

Cons:

1. Subjective Pattern Interpretation: Different traders may interpret chart patterns differently, leading to inconsistent trading decisions.

2. Pattern Failures in Volatile Markets: Chart patterns can fail in volatile markets, resulting in losing trades.

Key Points

1. Position Sizing: Allocate 1-2% of the trading account per trade.

2. Stop Loss Placement: Place a stop loss 2-3 Average True Range (ATR) away from the entry point to manage risk.

3. Take Profit Target: Set a take profit target 1-2 ATR away from the entry point to lock in profits.

4. Suitable Pairs: This strategy can be applied to any currency pair.

5. Timing: Enter trades when chart patterns are forming.

Indeed pattern trading is a viable strategy for forex traders. However, traders should note the potential for subjective pattern interpretation and the possibility of pattern failures in volatile markets.

| 31. SCALPING WITH LIMIT ORDERS

| Use limit orders to scalp the market. | Can be profitable in volatile markets. | Requires fast reaction times, can be stressful. | 0.5-1% of account | 10-20 pips | 10-20 pips | Volatile pairs, e.g., EUR/USD, GBP/USD | High volatility periods |

Interpretation

1. Strategy: This strategy involves using limit orders to scalp the forex market. Limit orders allow traders to specify the exact price at which they want to buy or sell a currency pair.

2. Profitability: Scalping with limit orders can be a profitable strategy, especially in volatile markets. When the market moves quickly, there are often opportunities to catch small profits by scalping price movements.

3. Requirements: Successful scalping requires fast reaction times and the ability to make quick decisions. It can also be a stressful trading approach, as traders need to be constantly monitoring the market and making trades.

4. Risk: Scalping is a high-risk trading strategy. Traders should only risk a small percentage of their account on each trade

(0.5-1%).

5. Profit Target: Scalpers typically aim for small profits, such as 10-20 pips per trade.

6. Stop Loss: It is important to use stop-loss orders with scalping to limit the risk of losses. Scalpers typically place their stop-loss orders just below (for long trades) or just above (for short trades) the entry price.

7. Best Currency Pairs: Volatile currency pairs, such as EUR/USD or GBP/USD, are good choices for scalping. These pairs tend to move quickly and offer more opportunities for scalping profits.

8. Best Trading Conditions: High volatility periods, such as news releases or economic data announcements, are ideal for scalping. During these times, the market is more likely to move quickly and offer more opportunities for profitable trades.

| 32. DAY TRADING WITH TRAILING STOP

| Use a trailing stop to protect profits as the market moves in your favor. | Can be profitable in trending markets. | Requires a lot of time and attention, can be stressful. | 1-2% of account | 2-3 ATR | 1-2 ATR | Trending pairs, e.g., EUR/USD, GBP/USD | During the day |

A trailing stop is a dynamic stop-loss order that moves with the market in order to protect profits while allowing a trade to remain open and continue to profit. It is designed to lock in profits as the market moves in your favor and exit the trade if the market turns against you.

Trailing Stop Benefits:

1. Profit Protection: A trailing stop automatically adjusts the stop-loss level as the market moves in your favor, ensuring that you lock in profits if the market reverses.

2. Extended Profit Potential: By allowing the trade to remain open while the market is trending in your favor, a trailing stop provides the opportunity for additional profits.

3. Reduced Risk: A trailing stop limits your downside risk by automatically exiting the trade if the market moves against you

beyond a predefined level.

Trailing Stop Considerations:

1. Time and Attention: Day trading with a trailing stop requires a significant amount of time and attention to monitor the market and adjust the stop-loss level accordingly.

2. Stress Level: Day trading with a trailing stop can be stressful, especially during volatile market conditions.

3. Risk Management: It is essential to set the trailing stop at a level that balances profit protection with the potential for extended profits.

Recommended Settings:

1. Account Size: Start with a small portion (1-2%) of your trading account to minimize potential losses.

2. Average True Range (ATR): Use an ATR of 2-3 times the ATR as a starting point. Adjust it based on market volatility.

3. Initial Stop Loss: Set the initial stop loss at a level that provides a reasonable buffer for potential market fluctuations.

4. Currency Pairs: Choose trending currency pairs, such as EUR/USD or GBP/USD, for day trading with a trailing stop.

5. Trading Hours: Day trade during the most liquid and volatile hours of the day to maximize trading opportunities.

| 33. SWING TRADING WITH MULTIPLE ENTRIES

| Enter a trade in multiple tranches, adding to your position as the trade moves in your favor. | Can be profitable in trending markets. | Requires patience, can be difficult to identify good entry points. | 2-3% of account | 3-5 ATR | 2-3 ATR | Trending pairs, e.g., EUR/USD, GBP/USD | During a trend |

Pros:

Profitable in Trending Markets: This strategy can be effective in trending markets, as it allows traders to add to their positions as the trend continues.

Can Magnify Profits: By adding to a winning trade, traders can potentially magnify their profits.

Cons:

Requires Patience: This strategy requires patience, as traders need to wait for the right entry points to add to their positions.

Difficult to Identify Good Entry Points: Determining the optimal time to add to a position can be challenging, especially for inexperienced traders.

Riskier Than Single-Entry Trades: Adding to a position increases the trader's exposure to risk, making this strategy riskier than single-entry trades.

Implementation:

Risk Management: Swing trading with multiple entries can be risky, so it is essential to employ proper risk management techniques. Traders should use stop-loss orders to protect their capital and limit their losses.

Position Sizing: The size of each tranche should be carefully considered. The trader should start with a small position and add to it as the trade moves in their favor.

Exit Strategy: Traders should have a clear exit strategy before entering a trade. This will help them determine when to take profits or cut losses.

Recommended Parameters:

Risk: Traders should risk no more than 2-3% of their account on each trade.

Stop Loss: Traders should place their stop-loss orders at least 2-3 ATRs (average true ranges) away from their entry price.

Take Profit: Traders should have a take-profit target of at least 3-5 ATRs.

Suitable Pairs: This strategy is best suited for trending pairs like EUR/USD, GBP/USD, etc.

Best Time to Trade: Traders should look for trades during a trend, as this is when the strategy is most likely to be profitable.

| 34. HEDGING WITH OPTIONS

| Use options to hedge your positions. | Can be used to reduce risk. | Options can be complex and risky. | 1-2% of account | 2-3 ATR | 1-2 ATR | Any pair | When risk is high |

Considerations on this strategy:

Strategy Overview: This strategy utilizes options to hedge positions, aiming to reduce risk while still potentially profiting from market movements.

Key Points

- A specific percentage of the account balance (1-2%) is allocated for options trading.

- Options with 2-3 times the Average True Range (ATR) are suitable for this strategy.

- The stop loss is set at 1-2 times the ATR, providing a buffer against adverse price movements.

- The strategy can be applied to any currency pair, offering flexibility.

- This strategy is best employed when the market risk is high, as it seeks to mitigate potential losses.

- Advantages:

- Risk Reduction: Options provide a way to hedge positions

and limit potential losses.

- Profit Potential: Even with hedging, there is still the potential to profit from market movements.

- Flexibility: The strategy can be applied to any currency pair, allowing traders to diversify their portfolio.

Disadvantages:

- Complexity: Options trading can be complex and requires a deep understanding of options mechanics and risk management.

- Risk: Options trading involves inherent risk, and losses can exceed the initial investment.

- Cost: Options trading involves fees and commissions, which can eat into profits.

Hedging with options can be a valuable strategy for experienced traders seeking to reduce risk while still profiting from market movements. However, it's crucial to understand the complexities and risks associated with options trading before employing this strategy.

| 35. TREND FOLLOWING WITH MULTIPLE CURRENCY PAIRS

| Trade multiple currency pairs in the same direction. | Can be profitable if the trends are correlated. | Correlation can change, can be whipsawed if the correlations break down. | 1-2% of account | 2-3 ATR | 1-2 ATR | Trending pairs, e.g., EUR/USD, GBP/USD | Follow the trend |

One of the strategies that can be used in forex trading is trend following with multiple currency pairs. This strategy involves trading several pairs that have similar trends, such as EUR/USD and GBP/USD, in the same direction. The advantage of this strategy is that it can be profitable if the trends are strong and correlated, meaning that they move in the same way. However, the drawback of this strategy is that the correlation can change over time, and the pairs can diverge or reverse their trends. This can lead to losses if the trader does not exit the trades quickly or use stop losses. A recommended risk management for this strategy is to risk 1-2% of the account per trade, use a 2-3 ATR trailing stop loss, and target a 1-2 ATR profit. The trader should also look for pairs that have clear and consistent trends, and follow the trend direction until it changes.

| 36. COUNTER-TREND TRADING WITH MULTIPLE TIMEFRAMES

| Use multiple timeframes to identify potential reversals in the market and then trade against the trend on a shorter timeframe. | Can be profitable in ranging markets. | Can be difficult to identify reversals, can be whipsawed in trending markets. | 1-2% of account | 2-3 ATR | 1-2 ATR | Range-bound pairs, e.g., EUR/JPY, GBP/JPY | Near potential reversals |

Counter-Trend Trading with Multiple Timeframes is a strategy that aims to exploit the fluctuations in the market that go against the dominant trend. This strategy requires the use of multiple timeframes to identify the points where the market is likely to reverse and then enter a trade in the opposite direction of the trend on a lower timeframe. For example, if the daily chart shows a downtrend, the trader would look for a bullish reversal on the 4-hour or 1-hour chart and then go long on the 15-minute or 5-minute chart. This strategy can be profitable in markets that are ranging or consolidating, as it can capture the swings within the range. However, this strategy can also be risky and challenging, as it can be hard to spot reliable reversal signals and the trader can face frequent losses in markets that are strongly trending. Therefore, this strategy requires strict risk management and discipline. The trader should only risk 1-2% of their account per trade, set a stop-loss at 2-3 times the average true range (ATR) of the lower timeframe, and take profits at 1-2 times the ATR. This strategy is suitable for pairs that tend to move sideways, such as EUR/JPY and GBP/JPY. The best time to apply this strategy is when the market is near potential reversal zones, such as support and resistance levels, trendlines, Fibonacci retracements, or moving averages.

| 37. CARRY TRADE WITH MULTIPLE CURRENCY PAIRS

| Carry trade multiple currency pairs with a positive interest rate differential. | Can be profitable if the interest rate differentials are large enough. | Currency risk, interest rate risk. | 1-2% of account | 2-3 ATR | 1-2 ATR | Pairs with a large interest rate differential, e.g., AUD/JPY, NZD/JPY | When the interest rate differential is large |

A carry trade is a strategy that involves borrowing a low-interest currency and investing in a high-interest currency. The aim is to profit from the difference in interest rates, as well as any appreciation in the value of the high-interest currency. A carry trade can be done with multiple currency pairs, as long as there is a positive interest rate differential between them. For example, one can borrow Japanese yen (JPY), which has a low interest rate, and invest in Australian dollars (AUD) or New Zealand dollars (NZD), which have higher interest rates.

The potential profit of a carry trade depends on the size of the interest rate differential, as well as the exchange rate movements. If the interest rate differential is large enough, the carry trade can be profitable even if the exchange rate does not change or moves slightly against the trader. However, there are also risks involved in a carry trade, such as currency risk and interest rate risk. Currency risk is the possibility that the exchange rate moves unfavorably for the trader, wiping out the interest income or causing a capital loss. Interest rate risk is the possibility that the interest rates change unexpectedly, narrowing the interest rate differential or reversing it.

To implement a carry trade with multiple currency pairs, one needs to select the pairs that have a large interest rate differential and are likely to maintain it for a long time. Some examples are AUD/JPY and NZD/JPY, which have historically had high interest rate differentials. One also needs to determine the position size, the stop loss level, and the take profit level for each pair. A common rule of thumb is to risk no more than 1-2% of the account balance per trade, and to set the stop loss and take profit at 2-3 times and 1-2 times the average true range (ATR) of the pair, respectively. The ATR is a measure of volatility that reflects how much the price moves on average over a given period of time.

The best time to enter a carry trade with multiple currency pairs is when the interest rate differential is large and stable, and when the exchange rate trend is favorable for the trader. For example, if one expects the AUD or NZD to appreciate against the JPY, then it would be a good time to buy AUD/JPY or NZD/JPY. Conversely, if one expects the JPY to appreciate against the AUD or NZD, then it would be a bad time to enter a carry trade with these pairs.

| 38. FOREX ROBOTS WITH MULTIPLE STRATEGIES

| Use a forex robot that employs multiple trading strategies. | Can be profitable if the strategies are complementary. | Forex robots can be expensive, can be difficult to set up and manage. | 1-2% of account | 2-3 ATR | 1-2 ATR | Any pair | 24/5 |

If you want to trade forex without spending too much time or effort, you might want to consider using a forex robot that employs multiple trading strategies. A forex robot is a software program that automatically executes trades based on predefined rules and indicators. A forex robot that uses multiple strategies can adapt to different market conditions and increase your chances of making profits. However, there are also some drawbacks to using a forex robot with multiple strategies. For one thing, you need to make sure that the strategies are complementary and not contradictory. For example, you don't want a robot that buys and sells the same pair at the same time. Also, you need to be aware that forex robots can be expensive, can be difficult to set up and manage, and can have technical glitches or errors. Therefore, you should only use a forex robot with multiple strategies if you have enough experience and knowledge in forex trading, and if you are willing to monitor and adjust your robot regularly.

Some general guidelines for using a forex robot with multiple strategies are:

- Risk only 1-2% of your account per trade. This will help you avoid losing too much money if the robot makes a wrong decision or if the market moves against you.

- Set your stop loss at 2-3 ATR (average true range) below or above the entry price. This will protect your capital from large price swings and volatility.

- Set your take profit at 1-2 ATR above or below the entry price. This will help you lock in some profits and avoid being greedy.

- Trade any pair that has good liquidity and low spreads. This will reduce your trading costs and increase your profitability.

- Trade 24/5, which is the standard operating time of the forex market. This will allow you to take advantage of all the trading opportunities and signals that the robot generates.

Here are some key factors to consider:

1. Robustness and Adaptability:

   - A decent trading robot should be robust and adaptable to changing market conditions. It should be able to handle unexpected events, such as sudden price fluctuations, news releases, or economic shifts.

   - Money management parameters, while important, cannot account for all possible market scenarios. A robot that is overly sensitive to market noise or fails to adjust its strategy based on market dynamics is likely to encounter difficulties over time.

2. Quality of Trading Signals:

   - The effectiveness of a trading robot largely depends on the quality of the trading signals it generates. These signals should be based on reliable technical indicators, fundamental analysis, or other sound trading strategies.

- Money management can help optimize the execution of these signals, but it cannot improve their accuracy or profitability. Poorly designed trading signals will inevitably lead to subpar results, regardless of the money management strategy employed.

3. Risk Management:

- Money management is a crucial aspect of trading, as it helps control and mitigate financial risks. However, it is only one part of a comprehensive risk management strategy.

- A decent trading robot should incorporate features such as stop-loss orders, position sizing, and diversification to manage risk effectively. Money management parameters should be integrated with these risk management tools to create a holistic approach to risk mitigation.

4. Overfitting and Optimization:

- Trading robots are often optimized and tested on historical data to achieve the best possible performance. However, this process can lead to overfitting, where the robot learns the specific patterns in the historical data but fails to generalize well to new, unseen market conditions.

- Money management parameters cannot compensate for overfitting. Instead, it is essential to ensure that the trading robot is properly validated on out-of-sample data or through rigorous cross-validation techniques to mitigate the risk of overfitting.

5. Human Intervention and Oversight:

- Trading robots, even the best ones, are not perfect. They

can malfunction, make mistakes, or encounter unforeseen challenges.

- Human intervention and oversight are crucial to ensure that the trading robot is functioning properly, adapting to changing market conditions, and generating profitable signals.

- Money management parameters alone cannot replace the role of human judgment and discretion in monitoring and managing the trading robot's performance.

Indeed, while money management parameters play a vital role in the profitability of a trading robot, they are not the sole determinant of success. A decent trading robot should possess robustness, adaptability, high-quality trading signals, effective risk management strategies, and be validated against overfitting. Ultimately, the effectiveness of a trading robot depends on a combination of factors, including money management, trading signal quality, risk management, and human oversight.

Now let's explore a trading bot for Meta Trader, a common trading platform with its own Meta Editor. Note: this is a working example that can be customized.

First, Let's Explain, Line By Line This Mql4 Script/ Expert Advisor

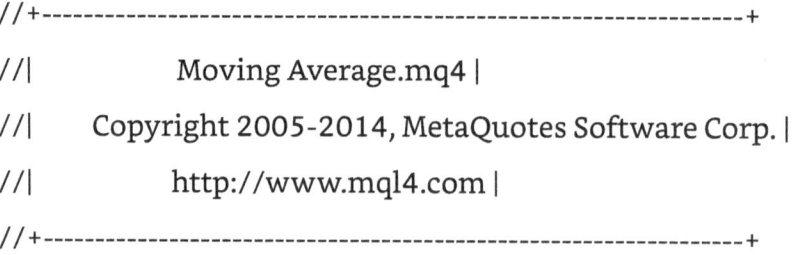

```
//+------------------------------------------------------------------+
//|                        Moving Average.mq4 |
//|      Copyright 2005-2014, MetaQuotes Software Corp. |
//|                        http://www.mql4.com |
//+------------------------------------------------------------------+
```

```
#property copyright "2005-2014, MetaQuotes Software Corp."
#property link   "http://www.mql4.com"
#property description "Moving Average sample expert advisor"

#define MAGICMA 20131111
//--- Inputs
input double Lots    =0.1;
input double MaximumRisk =0.02;
input double DecreaseFactor=3;
input int  MovingPeriod =12;
input int  MovingShift =6;
//+------------------------------------------------------------------+
//| Calculate open positions          |
//+------------------------------------------------------------------+
int CalculateCurrentOrders(string symbol)
{
  int buys=0,sells=0;
//---
  for(int i=0;i<OrdersTotal();i++)
    {
    if(OrderSelect(i,SELECT_BY_POS,MODE_TRADES)==false)
break;
    if(OrderSymbol()==Symbol()                        &&
OrderMagicNumber()==MAGICMA)
      {
      if(OrderType()==OP_BUY) buys++;
```

```
      if(OrderType()==OP_SELL) sells++;
     }
    }
//--- return orders volume
  if(buys>0) return(buys);
  else   return(-sells);
}
//+----------------------------------------------------------------+
//| Calculate optimal lot size          |
//+----------------------------------------------------------------+
double LotsOptimized()
{
  double lot=Lots;
  int  orders=HistoryTotal();  // history orders total
  int  losses=0;     // number of losses orders without a break
//--- select lot size
  lot=NormalizeDouble(AccountFreeMargin()*MaximumRisk/1000.0,1);
//--- calcuulate number of losses orders without a break
  if(DecreaseFactor>0)
   {
   for(int i=orders-1;i>=0;i--)
    {
    if(OrderSelect(i,SELECT_BY_POS,MODE_HISTORY)==false)
     {
     Print("Error in history!");
```

```
      break;
      }
    if(OrderSymbol()!=Symbol() || OrderType()>OP_SELL)
      continue;
    //---
    if(OrderProfit()>0) break;
    if(OrderProfit()<0) losses++;
    }
  if(losses>1)
    lot=NormalizeDouble(lot-lot*losses/DecreaseFactor,1);
  }
//--- return lot size
  if(lot<0.1) lot=0.1;
  return(lot);
}
//+ --------------------------------------------------------------+
//| Check for open order conditions        |
//+--------------------------------------------------------------+
void CheckForOpen()
{
  double ma;
  int res;
//--- go trading only for first tiks of new bar
  if(Volume[0]>1) return;
//--- get Moving Average
  ma=iMA(NULL,0,MovingPeriod,MovingShift,MODE_SMA,PRIC
```

```
E_CLOSE,0);
//--- sell conditions
  if(Open[1]>ma && Close[1]<ma)
    {
    res=OrderSend(Symbol(),OP_SELL,LotsOptimized(),Bid,3,0,0,
"",MAGICMA,0,Red);
    return;
    }
//--- buy conditions
  if(Open[1]<ma && Close[1]>ma)
    {
    res=OrderSend(Symbol(),OP_BUY,LotsOptimized(),Ask,3,0,0,"
",MAGICMA,0,Blue);
    return;
    }
//---
}
//+------------------------------------------------------------------+
//| Check for close order conditions        |
//+------------------------------------------------------------------+
void CheckForClose()
{
  double ma;
//--- go trading only for first tiks of new bar
  if(Volumc[0]>1) return;
//--- get Moving Average
```

```
   ma=iMA(NULL,0,MovingPeriod,MovingShift,MODE_SMA,PRIC
E_CLOSE,0);
//---
  for(int i=0;i<OrdersTotal();i++)
   {
   if(OrderSelect(i,SELECT_BY_POS,MODE_TRADES)==false)
break;
   if(OrderMagicNumber()!=MAGICMA    ||    OrderSymbol()!
=Symbol()) continue;
    //--- check order type
    if(OrderType()==OP_BUY)
    {
     if(Open[1]>ma && Close[1]<ma)
      {
      if(!OrderClose(OrderTicket(),OrderLots(),Bid,3,White))
        Print("OrderClose error ",GetLastError());
      }
     break;
    }
    if(OrderType()==OP_SELL)
    {
     if(Open[1]<ma && Close[1]>ma)
      {
      if(!OrderClose(OrderTicket(),OrderLots(),Ask,3,White))
        Print("OrderClose error ",GetLastError());
      }
```

```
      break;
    }
  }
//---
}
//+------------------------------------------------------------------+
//| OnTick function                  |
//+------------------------------------------------------------------+
void OnTick()
{
//--- check for history and trading
  if(Bars<100 || IsTradeAllowed()==false)
    return;
//--- calculate open orders by current symbol
  if(CalculateCurrentOrders(Symbol())==0) CheckForOpen();
  else          CheckForClose();
//---
}
//+------------------------------------------------------------------+
```

* The first few lines are standard MQL4 header comments, containing information about the expert advisor, its copyright, and link to the MQL4 website.

* #property copyright "2005-2014, MetaQuotes Software Corp."

* #property link   "http://www.mql4.com"

* #property description "Moving Average sample expert advisor"

* The next lines define a few constants and input parameters:

* #define MAGICMA 20131111 – defines the magic number for orders placed by this expert advisor.

* input double Lots   =0.1; – the initial lot size for trades.

* input double MaximumRisk =0.02; – the maximum risk per trade, expressed as a percentage of the account balance.

* input double DecreaseFactor=3; – the factor by which to decrease the lot size after a certain number of consecutive losses.

* input int   MovingPeriod =12; – the period of the moving average.

* input int MovingShift =6; – the shift of the moving average.

The following functions are defined:

* CalculateCurrentOrders(string symbol): calculates the number of open orders for the specified symbol.

* LotsOptimized(): calculates the optimal lot size for the current market conditions, taking into account the maximum risk and the number of consecutive losses.

* CheckForOpen(): checks if there are any open orders for the current symbol and, if not, places a new order based on the moving average.

* CheckForClose(): checks if there are any open orders for the current symbol and, if so, closes them if the moving average has crossed the opposite side of the price.

* OnTick(): the main function of the expert advisor, which is called every time a new tick is received. It checks if there are enough bars of history data and if trading is allowed, and then calls the CheckForOpen() and CheckForClose() functions.

What's The Best Time Frame For Trading With This Moving Average?

The provided code does not specify a preferred timeframe for trading with the moving average strategy. The selection of the timeframe depends on the trader's risk tolerance, trading style, and the characteristics of the financial instrument being traded.

For example, a trader might choose to use a shorter timeframe, such as the 1-minute or 5-minute chart, for scalping or day trading, where positions are held for a short period of time. In this case, the trader would need to be more responsive to price fluctuations and would need to manage their risk carefully.

On the other hand, a trader might choose to use a longer timeframe, such as the daily or weekly chart, for swing trading or long-term investments. In this case, the trader would be less concerned with short-term price fluctuations and would focus on identifying longer-term trends and potential trading opportunities.

Ultimately, the best timeframe for trading with a moving average strategy depends on the individual trader's preferences and trading style, and there is no one-size-fits-all answer. Traders should experiment with different timeframes and back test their strategies to determine what works best for them.

How Many Moving Averages Are There?

The provided code uses only one moving average.

It is calculated using the iMA() function with the following parameters:

* NULL: specifies that the moving average should be calculated on the current symbol.

* 0: specifies that the moving average should be calculated on the Close price.

* MovingPeriod: specifies the period of the moving average.

* MovingShift: specifies the shift of the moving average.

* MODE_SMA: specifies that the moving average should be calculated using the Simple Moving Average (SMA) method.

Therefore, the code uses a single Simple Moving Average with the specified period and shift.

Let's Define Movingshift

The *MovingShift* input parameter in the provided code specifies the number of bars to shift the moving average forward or backward.

A positive value shifts the moving average forward, which means that the moving average will be calculated using more recent data. This can make the moving average more responsive to price changes, but it can also make it more volatile and prone to false signals.

A negative value shifts the moving average backward, which means that the moving average will be calculated using older data. This can make the moving average less responsive to price changes, but it can also make it smoother and less volatile.

The optimal value for the *MovingShift* parameter depends on the specific trading strategy and the characteristics of the financial instrument being traded. Traders should experiment with different values to determine what works best for them.

In the provided code, the *MovingShift* parameter is set to 6, which means that the moving average is shifted forward by 6 bars. This value is relatively conservative and should help to reduce the volatility of the moving average and make it less prone to false signals. However, traders may want to experiment with different values to see if they can improve the performance of the strategy.

If timeframe of 15 minute is chosen, what's the recommended shift and MA? When choosing a timeframe of 15 minutes for trading with a moving average strategy, the recommended shift and MA period depend on the specific trading strategy and the characteristics of the financial instrument being traded. However, a good starting point is to use a relatively short period for the moving average, such as 10 or 20 periods, and a shift of 0 or 1.

This will help to reduce the volatility of the moving average and make it less prone to false signals. However, traders may want to experiment with different values to see if they can improve the performance of the strategy.

For example, if the trader is using a scalping strategy, they may want to use a shorter period for the moving average, such as 5 or 10 periods, and a shift of 0 or 1. This will make the moving average more responsive to price changes, but it may also make it more volatile.

On the other hand, if the trader is using a swing trading strategy, they may want to use a longer period for the moving average, such as 20 or 50 periods, and a shift of 0 or 1. This will make the moving average less responsive to price changes, but it may also make it smoother and less volatile.

Ultimately, the best shift and MA period for a 15-minute timeframe will depend on the individual trader's preferences and trading style. Traders should experiment with different values and back test their strategies to determine what works best for them.

Here Are Some Additional Tips For Choosing The Shift And Ma Period For A 15-Minute Timeframe

* Consider the volatility of the financial instrument being traded. More volatile instruments may require a shorter period for the moving average.

* Consider the trading style. Scalpers may want to use a shorter period, while swing traders may want to use a longer period.

* Experiment with different values to see what works best for you. Back testing your strategies with different shift and MA period values can help you to identify the optimal settings for your particular trading style.

"I Wonder Why A Period Of 12 Was Chosen"

The choice of a 12-period moving average in the provided code is likely based on a combination of factors, including:

Commonly used period: The 12-period moving average is a commonly used setting for moving average strategies in technical analysis. It is long enough to smooth out short-term price fluctuations while still being responsive to changes in the underlying trend.

Balance between responsiveness and smoothness: A 12-period moving average provides a balance between responsiveness and smoothness. It is not so short that it is too volatile and prone to false signals, but it is not so long that it lags behind the price action.

Back testing and optimization: The 12-period moving average may have been chosen based on back testing and optimization of the strategy. The trader may have found that the 12-period moving average produced the best results in terms of profitability and risk-adjusted returns.

It is important to note that the optimal moving average period can vary depending on the specific trading strategy, the characteristics of the financial instrument being traded, and the market conditions. Traders should experiment with different moving average periods and back test their strategies to determine what works best for them.

Here are some additional reasons why a 12-period moving average might have been chosen:

Simplicity: The 12-period moving average is a simple and straightforward indicator to use. It is easy to calculate and interpret, even for beginner traders.

Robustness: The 12-period moving average is a relatively robust indicator. It is not as sensitive to outliers or extreme price movements as some other indicators, such as the Bollinger

Bands or the Relative Strength Index (RSI).

Versatility: The 12-period moving average can be used in a variety of trading strategies, including trend following, swing trading, and scalping. It can also be used to identify support and resistance levels, and to confirm trading signals from other indicators.

Indeed the 12-period moving average is a popular choice for moving average strategies due to its simplicity, robustness, and versatility. However, traders should always experiment with different moving average periods and back test their strategies to determine what works best for them.

Why a *MovingShift* of 6? The choice of a *MovingShift* of 6 in the provided code is likely based on a combination of factors, including:

Smoothing: A *MovingShift* of 6 can help to smooth out the moving average and make it less prone to false signals. This is because the moving average will be calculated using data from a wider range of bars.

Responsiveness: A *MovingShift* of 6 can also help to keep the moving average responsive to changes in the underlying trend. This is because the moving average will not be lagging behind the price action as much.

 Back testing and optimization: The *MovingShift* of 6 may have been chosen based on back testing and optimization of the strategy. The trader may have found that the *MovingShift* of 6 produced the best results in terms of profitability and risk-adjusted returns.

It is important to note that the optimal *MovingShift*

can vary depending on the specific trading strategy, the characteristics of the financial instrument being traded, and the market conditions. Traders should experiment with different *MovingShift* values and back test their strategies to determine what works best for them.

Here are some additional reasons why a *MovingShift* of 6 might have been chosen:

Commonly used setting: A *MovingShift* of 6 is a commonly used setting for moving average strategies in technical analysis. It is a relatively conservative setting that helps to smooth out the moving average without making it too laggy.

Balance between smoothness and responsiveness: A *MovingShift* of 6 provides a balance between smoothness and responsiveness. It is not so large that the moving average is too smooth and unresponsive to changes in the underlying trend, but it is not so small that the moving average is too volatile and prone to false signals.

Versatility: A *MovingShift* of 6 can be used in a variety of trading strategies, including trend following, swing trading, and scalping. It can also be used to identify support and resistance levels, and to confirm trading signals from other indicators.

Overall, a *MovingShift* of 6 is a popular choice for moving average strategies due to its balance between smoothness and responsiveness, as well as its versatility. However, traders should always experiment with different *MovingShift* values and back test their strategies to determine what works best for them.

What's The Best Pair To Trade With This Code?

The best pair to trade with the provided code depends on a number of factors, including:

Volatility: The pair should be volatile enough to generate trading opportunities, but not so volatile that it is difficult to manage risk.

Trend: The pair should be trending, as the strategy is designed to follow the trend.

Liquidity: The pair should be liquid enough to ensure that orders can be executed quickly and at a fair price.

Correlation: The pair should not be highly correlated with other pairs, as this can increase the risk of losses.

Some popular pairs that are often traded with moving average strategies include:

EUR/USD

GBP/USD

USD/JPY

AUD/USD

USD/CHF

EUR/JPY

GBP/JPY

AUD/JPY

NZD/USD

USD/CAD

Traders should also consider their own risk tolerance and

trading style when choosing a pair to trade. For example, a trader with a low risk tolerance may want to choose a less volatile pair, while a trader with a more aggressive trading style may want to choose a more volatile pair.

Ultimately, the best pair to trade with the provided code will depend on the individual trader's preferences and trading style. Traders should experiment with different pairs and back test their strategies to determine what works best for them.

Here are some additional tips for choosing the best pair to trade with the provided code:

Consider the current market conditions. Some pairs may be more or less volatile than usual, depending on economic and political events.

Monitor the pair's historical volatility. This can help you to identify pairs that are more or less volatile than average.

Back test your strategy on different pairs. This can help you to see how the strategy performs on different pairs and to identify pairs that are more profitable.

Consider your own risk tolerance and trading style. Choose a pair that is appropriate for your risk tolerance and trading style.

By following these tips, you can increase your chances of success when trading with the provided code.

What's the best way to improve this code? There are a few ways to improve the provided code:

Add more technical indicators: The current code only uses a single moving average. Adding more technical indicators, such as the Relative Strength Index (RSI), the Bollinger Bands, or the Stochastic Oscillator, can help to improve the accuracy of the trading signals.

Optimize the input parameters: The current code uses a fixed set of input parameters. However, these parameters can be optimized to improve the performance of the strategy. For example, the trader could experiment with different moving average periods and shifts, as well as different settings for the *MaximumRisk* and *DecreaseFactor* parameters.

Add a stop loss: The current code does not include a stop loss. Adding a stop loss can help to protect the trader from losses if the trade goes against them.

Add a take profit: The current code does not include a take profit. Adding a take profit can help to lock in profits when the trade goes in the trader's favor.

Use a more sophisticated money management system: The current code uses a simple money management system that allocates a fixed lot size to each trade. A more sophisticated money management system, such as the Kelly criterion or the fixed fractional position sizing method, can help to improve the profitability of the strategy.

Back test the strategy: The current code has not been back tested. Back testing the strategy can help to identify potential weaknesses and to optimize the input parameters.

Here are some additional tips for improving the provided code:

Use a programming language that is designed for trading: There are a number of programming languages that are specifically designed for trading, such as Python, R, and C++. These languages have built-in libraries that make it easy to develop and test trading strategies.

Use a trading platform that supports automated trading: There are a number of trading platforms that support automated trading, such as MetaTrader 4, MetaTrader 5, and cTrader. These platforms allow traders to develop and deploy trading strategies without having to write any code.

Get help from a professional: If you are new to trading or if you are not sure how to improve your trading strategy, you may want to get help from a professional trader or a financial advisor.

By following these tips, you can improve the performance of the provided code and develop a more profitable trading strategy.

Let's Add A Stop Loss And Take Profit

To add a stop loss and take profit to the provided code, you can use the following steps:

1. Add two new input parameters for the stop loss and take profit levels. For example:

StopLoss = 20; // Stop loss level in pips
input double TakeProfit = 50; // Take profit level in pips

2. Calculate the stop loss and take profit levels for each trade. For example:

= Bid - StopLoss * Point;
double takeProfit = Ask + TakeProfit * Point;

3. Add the stop loss and take profit levels to the OrderSend() function. For example:

```
=OrderSend(Symbol(),OP_SELL,LotsOptimized(),Bid,3,stopLoss,
takeProfit,"",MAGICMA,0,Red);
```

4. Add a check to close the trade if the stop loss or take profit level is reached. For exam

```
// Add a new input parameter for the take profit level
input double TakeProfit = 50; // Take profit level in pips
```

```
// Calculate the take profit level for each trade
double takeProfit = Ask + TakeProfit * Point;
```

```
// Add the take profit level to the OrderSend() function
res=OrderSend(Symbol(),OP_SELL,LotsOptimized(),Bid,3,stopL
oss,takeProfit,"",MAGICMA,0,Red);
```

```
// Add a check to close the trade if the take profit level is reached
for(int i=0;i<OrdersTotal();i++)
{
  if(OrderSelect(i,SELECT_BY_POS,MODE_TRADES)==false)
break;
  if(OrderMagicNumber()!=MAGICMA    ||    OrderSymbol()!
=Symbol()) continue;
// Check if take profit level is reached
  if(OrderType()==OP_BUY)
  {
    if(Bid >= takeProfit)
    {
      if(!OrderClose(OrderTicket(),OrderLots(),Bid,3,White))
        Print("OrderClose error ",GetLastError());
    }
  }
```

```
  else if(OrderType()==OP_SELL)
  {
    if(Ask <= takeProfit)
    {
      if(!OrderClose(OrderTicket(),OrderLots(),Ask,3,White))
        Print("OrderClose error ",GetLastError());
    }
  }
}
```

` ` `

This code would close a trade if it reached either the stop loss level or the take profit level.

Here are some additional things to consider when using a take profit level:

* The take profit level should be set at a level that is realistic and achievable.

* The take profit level should be adjusted based on the current market conditions.

* The take profit level should be used in conjunction with a stop loss level to protect the trader from losses.

By following these tips, you can use a take profit level to improve the profitability of your trading strategy.

Now Let's Add Lines Of Code To Take Profit When The Net Value Of The Account Reaches 1 Percent

To add lines of code to take profit when the Net Value of the account reaches 1 percent, you can use the following steps:

1. Add a new input parameter for the Net Value percentage. For example:

```
` ` `
```

```
input double NetValuePercentage = 1; // Net Value percentage
` ` `
```

2. Calculate the Net Value of the account. For example:

```
` ` `
```

```
double netValue = AccountBalance() + AccountEquity();
` ` `
```

3. Check if the Net Value of the account has reached the specified percentage. For example:

```
` ` `
```

```
if(netValue >= AccountBalance() * (1 + NetValuePercentage / 100))
` ` `
```

4. Close all open orders if the Net Value of the account has reached the specified percentage. For example:

```
` ` `
```

```
for(int i=0;i<OrdersTotal();i++)
{
  if(OrderSelect(i,SELECT_BY_POS,MODE_TRADES)==false)
break;
  if(OrderMagicNumber()!=MAGICMA     ||     OrderSymbol()!
=Symbol()) continue;

  if(!OrderClose(OrderTicket(),OrderLots(),Bid,3,White))
    Print("OrderClose error ",GetLastError());
}
```

` ` `

Here is an example of how the code would look with these changes:

` ` `

```
//+------------------------------------------------------------------+
//|                    Moving Average.mq4 |
//|     Copyright 2005-2014, MetaQuotes Software Corp. |
//|               http://www.mql4.com |
//+------------------------------------------------------------------+
#property copyright "2005-2014, MetaQuotes Software Corp."
#property link   "http://www.mql4.com"
#property description "Moving Average sample expert advisor"

#define MAGICMA 20131111
//--- Inputs
input double Lots   =0.1;
```

```
input double MaximumRisk  =0.02;

input double DecreaseFactor=3;

input int  MovingPeriod =12;

input int  MovingShift  =6;

input double NetValuePercentage = 1; // Net Value percentage

//+--------------------------------------------------------------------+
//| Calculate open positions            |
//+--------------------------------------------------------------------+
int CalculateCurrentOrders(string symbol)
{
  int buys=0,sells=0;
//---
  for(int i=0;i<OrdersTotal();i++)
   {
   if(OrderSelect(i,SELECT_BY_POS,MODE_TRADES)==false) break;
   if(OrderSymbol()==Symbol()                          &&
OrderMagicNumber()==MAGICMA)
    {
    if(OrderType()==OP_BUY) buys++;
    if(OrderType()==OP_SELL) sells++;
    }
   }
//--- return orders volume
  if(buys>0) return(buys);
  else   return(-sells);
```

```
}
//+------------------------------------------------------------------+
//| Calculate optimal lot size        |
//+------------------------------------------------------------------+
double LotsOptimized()
{
  double lot=Lots;
  int  orders=HistoryTotal();  // history orders total
  int  losses=0;     // number of losses orders without a break
//--- select lot size
  lot=NormalizeDouble(AccountFreeMargin()*MaximumRisk/1000.0,1);
//--- calcuulate number of losses orders without a break
  if(DecreaseFactor>0)
   {
   for(int i=orders-1;i>=0;i--)
    {
    if(OrderSelect(i,SELECT_BY_POS,MODE_HISTORY)==false)
     {
     Print("Error in history!");
     break;
     }
    if(OrderSymbol()!=Symbol() || OrderType()>OP_SELL)
     continue;
    //---
    if(OrderProfit()>0) break;
```

```
      if(OrderProfit()<0) losses++;
    }
  if(losses>1)
    lot=NormalizeDouble(lot-lot*losses/DecreaseFactor,1);
  }
//--- return lot size
  if(lot<0.1) lot=0.1;
  return(lot);
}
//+------------------------------------------------------------------+
//| Check for open order conditions          |
//+------------------------------------------------------------------+
void CheckForOpen()
{
  double ma;
  int  res;
//--- go trading only for first tiks of new bar
  if(Volume[0]>1) return;
//--- get Moving Average
  ma=iMA(NULL,0,MovingPeriod,MovingShift,MODE_SMA,PRIC
E_CLOSE,0);
//--- sell conditions
  if(Open[1]>ma && Close[1]<ma)
    {
    res=OrderSend(Symbol(),OP_SELL,LotsOptimized(),Bid,3,0,0,
"",MAGICMA,0,Red);
```

```
    return;
    }
//--- buy conditions
  if(Open[1]<ma && Close[1]>ma)
    {
    res=OrderSend(Symbol(),OP_BUY,LotsOptimized(),Ask,3,0,0,"
",MAGICMA,0,Blue);
    return;
    }
//---
  }
//+------------------------------------------------------------------+
//| Check for close order conditions        |
//+------------------------------------------------------------------+
void CheckForClose()
  {
    double ma;
    double netValue = AccountBalance() + AccountEquity();
//--- go trading only for first tiks of new bar
    if(Volume[0]>1) return;
//--- get Moving Average
    ma=iMA(NULL,0,MovingPeriod,MovingShift,MODE_SMA,PRIC
E_CLOSE,0);
//---
    for(int i=0;i<OrdersTotal();i++)
      {
```

```
    if(OrderSelect(i,SELECT_BY_POS,MODE_TRADES)==false)
break;
    if(OrderMagicNumber()!=MAGICMA    ||    OrderSymbol()!
=Symbol()) continue;
    //--- check order type
    if(OrderType()==OP_BUY)
     {
      if(Open[1]>ma && Close[1]<ma)
       {
       if(!OrderClose(OrderTicket(),OrderLots(),Bid,3,White))
         Print("OrderClose error ",GetLastError());
       }
      break;
     }
    if(OrderType()==OP_SELL)
     {
      if(Open[1]<ma && Close[1]>ma)
       {
       if(!OrderClose(OrderTicket(),OrderLots(),Ask,3,White))
         Print("OrderClose error ",GetLastError());
       }
      break;
     }
    }
//--- check for Net Value
   if(netValue >= AccountBalance() * (1 + NetValuePercentage /
```

```
100))
  {
    for(int i=0;i<OrdersTotal();i++)
    {
      if(OrderSelect(i,SELECT_BY_POS,MODE_TRADES)==false)
break;
      if(OrderMagicNumber()!=MAGICMA  ||  OrderSymbol()!
=Symbol()) continue;

      if(!OrderClose(OrderTicket(),OrderLots(),Bid,3,White))
        Print("OrderClose error ",GetLastError());
    }
  }
//---
}
//+------------------------------------------------------------------+
//| OnTick function            |
//+------------------------------------------------------------------+
void OnTick()
{
//--- check for history and trading
  if(Bars<100 || IsTradeAllowed()==false)
    return;
//--- calculate open orders by current symbol
  if(CalculateCurrentOrders(Symbol())==0) CheckForOpen();
  else        CheckForClose();
```

```
//---

}

//+----------------------------------------------------------------+

` ` `
```

This code would close all open orders when the Net Value of the account reaches 1 percent above the initial account balance. If there's an error after compiling, copy the error including the line number of code and column into any AI IDE i.e. ChatGPT or Gemini (better), and cut and copy the code. This is the easiest way.

Please note that this is just an example, and you may need to adjust the code to fit your specific needs.

| 39. MOVING AVERAGES WITH MULTIPLE TIMEFRAMES

| Use multiple moving averages with different periods to identify trends and reversals. | Can be profitable in trending and ranging markets. | Moving averages can be lagging, can be whipsawed in choppy markets. | 1-2% of account | 2-3 ATR | 1-2 ATR | Any pair | 24/5 |

Moving averages are a popular tool for technical analysis. They smooth out the price data and show the direction and strength of a trend. By using multiple moving averages with different periods, you can get a better picture of the market situation and spot potential reversals. For example, you can use a 20-period moving average and a 50-period moving average on the same chart. When the 20-period moving average crosses above the 50-period moving average, it signals a bullish trend. When it crosses below, it signals a bearish trend. You can also use a third moving average with a longer period, such as 200, to confirm the overall trend.

This strategy can work well in both trending and ranging markets. In trending markets, you can follow the moving average crossover signals and ride the trend until it ends. In ranging markets, you can use the moving averages as support and resistance levels and trade the bounce. You can also use other indicators, such as RSI or MACD, to filter out false signals and identify divergences.

However, moving averages are not perfect. They are lagging indicators, which means they are based on past data and may not reflect the current market conditions. They can also be whipsawed in choppy markets, where the price moves back and forth without a clear direction. Therefore, you need to be careful with your risk management and exit strategy.

One way to manage your risk is to use a percentage of your account as your position size. For example, you can risk 1-2% of your account per trade. This way, you can limit your losses and protect your capital. Another way to manage your risk is to use ATR (average true range) as your stop loss and take profit levels. ATR measures the volatility of the market and adjusts to different timeframes. For example, you can use 2-3 ATR as your stop loss and 1-2 ATR as your take profit. This way, you can give your trade enough room to breathe and capture the most of the move.

You can apply this strategy to any currency pair and any timeframe. However, you may want to avoid trading during low liquidity periods, such as weekends or holidays, as the market may be more erratic and unpredictable. You may also want to avoid trading during major news events, as they may cause sudden spikes or reversals that can invalidate your signals.

Moving averages with multiple timeframes is a simple yet effective strategy that can help you identify trends and reversals in the forex market. By using different periods of moving averages, you can get a comprehensive view of the market situation and trade accordingly. By using proper risk management and exit strategy, you can increase your chances of success and profitability.

How To Find The Right Moving Average When Trading Multiple Pairs In Forex

1. Determine Your Trading Style:

   - Identify if you are a scalper, day trader, or swing trader.

2. Select a Timeframe:

   - Choose the timeframe that aligns with your trading style and pairs' volatility.

   - Common timeframes include 1-minute, 5-minute, 15-minute, 30-minute, 1-hour, and 4-hour charts.

3. Test Different Moving Averages:

   - Start with simple moving averages (SMA), exponential moving averages (EMA), or weighted moving averages (WMA).

   - Use different periods to see which one suits your strategy and the pairs you trade.

4. Analyze Historical Data:

   - Back test your moving average strategy on historical data of the pairs you trade.

   - This will help you understand how the moving average performed in various market conditions.

5. Monitor Market Volatility:

- Different currency pairs have different volatility levels.

- Adjust the period of your moving average based on the volatility of the pairs you trade.

- Use a shorter period for more volatile pairs and a longer period for less volatile pairs.

6. Consider Correlation:

- If you trade multiple correlated pairs, using the same moving average period may not be effective.

- Use different moving average periods for pairs that have different correlations.

7. Combine Moving Averages:

- Consider using multiple moving averages with different periods to create a more robust strategy.

- For example, you can use a short-term moving average for entry signals and a long-term moving average for trend confirmation.

8. Watch for False Signals:

- Moving averages can generate false signals, especially during volatile market conditions.

- Use other technical indicators to confirm your moving average signals.

9. Continuously Adapt:

- Monitor the performance of your moving average strategy regularly.

- Be open to adjusting the period of your moving average or testing new moving average types if needed.

Let's examine 3 scenarios:

Scenario 1: Scalping EUR/USD and GBP/USD:

- Trading Style: Scalping

- Timeframe: 1-minute or 5-minute chart

- Moving Average: Exponential Moving Average (EMA) with a period of 20 or 50

- Strategy: Use the EMA to identify short-term trends and potential reversal points. Look for trading opportunities when the price crosses above or below the EMA.

Scenario 2: Day Trading USD/JPY and AUD/USD:

- Trading Style: Day Trading

- Timeframe: 15-minute or 30-minute chart

- Moving Average: Simple Moving Average (SMA) with a period of 50 or 100

- Strategy: Use the SMA to determine the overall trend and support/resistance levels. Look for trading opportunities when the price bounces off the SMA or breaks through it.

Scenario 3: Swing Trading EUR/GBP and GBP/CHF:

- Trading Style: Swing Trading

- Timeframe: 4-hour or daily chart

- Moving Average: Weighted Moving Average (WMA) with a period of 200 or 300

- Strategy: Use the WMA to identify long-term trends and

potential turning points. Look for trading opportunities when the price crosses above the WMA to enter long positions and crosses below it to enter short positions.

Remember, these are just examples, and the specific moving average strategy that works best for you will depend on your trading style, the pairs you trade, and the market conditions. It is important to back test your strategy and monitor its performance continuously to make adjustments as needed.

For the record, I'm no big fan of back testing and prefer forward testing with a demo account with reliable data close enough to real trading—Oanda seems a good bet, from my side.

| 40. SUPPORT AND RESISTANCE WITH MULTIPLE TIMEFRAMES

| Use multiple support and resistance levels with different timeframes to identify potential trading opportunities. | Can be profitable in ranging markets. | Support and resistance levels can be broken, can be whipsawed in volatile markets. | 1-2% of account | 2-3 ATR | 1-2 ATR | Any pair | 24/5 | Tactic | Strategy | Pros | Cons | Position Sizing | Stop Loss | Take Profit | Appropriate Pair | Timing |

One possible tactic for trading in the forex market is to use multiple support and resistance levels with different timeframes to identify potential trading opportunities. Support and resistance levels are areas where the price tends to bounce or reverse, indicating a change in the market sentiment. By using different timeframes, such as daily, 4-hour, and 1-hour charts, you can find support and resistance levels that are relevant for different types of traders, such as long-term, medium-term, and short-term. This can help you to spot confluence zones, where multiple support and resistance levels align, creating stronger signals for entry and exit.

The strategy is suitable for ranging markets, where the price moves sideways within a defined range. By buying near the support level and selling near the resistance level, you can capture the price fluctuations and profit from the swings. The strategy can also be profitable in trending markets, if you use the support and resistance levels to confirm the trend direction and trade with the trend.

However, the strategy also has some drawbacks. Support and resistance levels are not fixed and can be broken by strong price movements. This can result in false signals or losses if the price moves against your position. Moreover, in volatile markets, the price can whipsaw between the support and resistance levels, creating noise and confusion. Therefore, it is important to use other indicators and tools, such as trend lines, moving averages, or Fibonacci retracements, to filter out the signals and confirm the validity of the support and resistance levels.

To manage your risk, you should use a position sizing method that limits your exposure to 1-2% of your account per trade. This means that you should adjust your lot size according to your stop loss distance and account balance. You should also use a stop loss order to protect your position from unexpected price movements. A reasonable stop loss level could be 2-3 ATR (average true range) away from the entry point, which reflects the volatility of the market. To lock in your profits, you should use a take profit order that is 1-2 ATR away from the entry point, which gives you a favorable risk-reward ratio.

The strategy can be applied to any currency pair, but it may work better on pairs that have lower spreads and higher liquidity, such as the major pairs or some of the crosses. The strategy can also be used at any time of the day or week, as long as there is enough market activity and volatility to create support and resistance levels. However, you should be aware of the news events and economic releases that can affect the market sentiment and cause sudden price movements.

| 41. BOLLINGER BANDS WITH MULTIPLE TIMEFRAMES

| Use multiple Bollinger Bands with different periods to identify overbought/oversold conditions. | Can be profitable in mean-reverting markets. | Bollinger Bands can be lagging, can be whipsawed in volatile markets. | 1% of account | 1-2 ATR | 1-2 ATR | Any pair | 24/5 |

Bollinger Bands are a technical indicator that consists of a moving average (usually 20 periods) and two standard deviations above and below it. The bands widen when the volatility increases and narrow when the volatility decreases. The idea is that the price is likely to revert to the mean when it reaches or exceeds the bands.

However, using only one Bollinger Band can be misleading, as the price can sometimes stay above or below the band for a long time, especially in trending markets. That's why I like to use multiple Bollinger Bands with different periods, such as 10, 20 and 50. This way, I can see the different levels of overbought/ oversold conditions and act accordingly.

Here's How I Use This Strategy

- I look for any currency pair that has low spreads and high liquidity. I prefer to trade on the 15-minute or 1-hour chart, but you can use any timeframe you like.

- I apply three Bollinger Bands with periods of 10, 20 and 50. I use the default settings of 2 standard deviations for each band.

- I wait for the price to touch or cross the outermost band (the 50-period one). This indicates a strong overbought/oversold condition.

- I then look for confirmation from the other two bands. If the price also touches or crosses the 20-period band, it's a stronger signal. If it also touches or crosses the 10-period band, it's an even stronger signal.

- I enter a trade in the opposite direction of the price movement, expecting a reversal to the mean. For example, if the price touches or crosses the upper band, I go short. If it touches or crosses the lower band, I go long.

- I risk 1% of my account per trade. I set my stop loss at 1-2 ATR (average true range) above or below the entry point, depending on whether I'm short or long. ATR is a measure of volatility that can help you adjust your stop loss according to the market conditions.

- I set my take profit at 1-2 ATR below or above the entry point, depending on whether I'm short or long. Alternatively, you can use a trailing stop or exit when the price reaches the middle band (the 20-period one).

- I trade this strategy 24/5, as long as there are no major news events that can affect the market.

| 42. ICHIMOKU KINKO HYO WITH MULTIPLE TIMEFRAMES

| Use multiple Ichimoku Kinko Hyo indicators with different periods to identify trends, turning points, and support and resistance levels. | Comprehensive trading system, can be profitable in trending and ranging markets. | Ichimoku Kinko Hyo can be complex, can be difficult to interpret signals. | 1-2% of account | 2-3 ATR | 1-2 ATR | Any pair | 24/5 |

Ichimoku Kinko Hyo, also known as the Ichimoku Cloud, is a comprehensive technical analysis tool that originated in Japan. It provides a holistic view of price action, combining multiple elements to help traders identify trends, turning points, and potential support and resistance levels. Let's break down the key aspects of Ichimoku Kinko Hyo with a focus on using it across multiple timeframes:

1. Components of Ichimoku Kinko Hyo:

   - Tenkan-sen (Conversion Line): This is the faster-moving line, calculated as the average of the highest high and lowest low over a specific period (usually 9 periods).

   - Kijun-sen (Base Line): The slower-moving line, calculated similarly to the Tenkan-sen but over a longer period (usually 26 periods).

- Senkou Span A (Leading Span A): Represents the midpoint between the Tenkan-sen and Kijun-sen, projected forward by 26 periods.

- Senkou Span B (Leading Span B): Calculated similarly to Senkou Span A but over an even longer period (usually 52 periods).

- Chikou Span (Lagging Span): Plots the closing price of the current candle shifted back by 26 periods.

2. Using Multiple Timeframes:

- Ichimoku Kinko Hyo is most effective when applied across different timeframes. By doing so, traders gain a more comprehensive perspective on price dynamics.

- Higher Timeframes (e.g., daily or weekly):

- Confirm the overall trend direction.

- Identify key support and resistance levels.

- Validate signals from lower timeframes.

- Lower Timeframes (e.g., 4-hour or 1-hour):

- Refine entry points.

- Fine-tune stop-loss and take-profit levels.

- Observe short-term price behavior.

3. Interpreting Signals:

- Bullish Signals:

- Price above the cloud (Senkou Span A and Senkou Span B).

- Tenkan-sen crosses above Kijun-sen.

- Chikou Span above historical price.

- Bearish Signals:

- Price below the cloud.

- Tenkan-sen crosses below Kijun-sen.

- Chikou Span below historical price.

4. Risk Management:

- Risk should be managed carefully:

- Allocate 1-2% of your account to each trade.

- Use ATR (Average True Range) to determine stop-loss levels.

- Consider the volatility of the currency pair.

- Trade during the 24/5 market hours.

| 43. CORRELATION TRADING WITH MULTIPLE CURRENCY PAIRS

| Correlate multiple currency
continue | Tactic | Strategy | Pros | Cons | Position Sizing | Stop Loss | Take Profit | Appropriate Pair | Timing |

Tactic

- Identify currency pairs with historically strong positive or negative correlations.

- Trade one currency pair while simultaneously taking a correlated position in the opposite direction in the other currency pair.

- Manage risk by keeping both positions relatively small in relation to your account size.

- Monitor the correlation between the two currency pairs on a daily basis.

Strategy

1. Choose Currency Pairs:

- Select currency pairs that have historically exhibited a strong and stable correlation. Examples include EUR/USD and GBP/USD, or USD/JPY and AUD/JPY.

2. Determine Correlation Strength:

- Calculate the correlation coefficient between the two pairs using historical data. A correlation coefficient close to 1 indicates a strong positive correlation, while a value close to -1 indicates a strong negative correlation.

3. Open Initial Position:

- In your chosen correlated pairs, open an initial position in a direction consistent with the historical correlation. For example, if EUR/USD and GBP/USD are positively correlated, you might buy EUR/USD and sell GBP/USD.

4. Monitor Correlation:

- Continuously monitor the correlation between the two currency pairs. If the correlation weakens or changes direction, adjust your positions accordingly.

5. Manage Risk:

- Maintain proper risk management by ensuring that both positions are relatively small relative to your account size. Use stop-loss orders to limit potential losses and protect your capital.

6. Take Profit:

- When the correlation between the two currency pairs begins to break down, consider taking profit and closing both positions. This will help you lock in your gains and avoid potential losses.

Pros:

- Diversification: This strategy can help diversify your portfolio by including multiple currency pairs with different correlation dynamics.

- Potential for Enhanced Returns: By exploiting the correlation between currency pairs, you may enhance your returns compared to trading a single currency pair.

- Flexibility: You can choose the correlation direction (positive or negative) based on your analysis and market conditions.

Cons:

- Correlation Risk: There is always the risk that the correlation between the currency pairs may change or even reverse, leading to potential losses.

- Market Volatility: This strategy can be sensitive to market volatility, and sudden shifts in market sentiment may impact the correlation between the pairs.

- Monitoring Requirement: It requires continuous monitoring of the correlation between the currency pairs to make timely adjustments to your positions.

Position Sizing:

- Both positions should be relatively small compared to your account size to manage risk effectively.

- Consider using a position size calculator to determine appropriate lot sizes based on your risk tolerance and account balance.

Stop Loss:

- Place stop-loss orders for both positions to limit potential losses in case the correlation between the currency pairs changes.

- The stop-loss levels should be strategically placed based on technical analysis or predetermined risk parameters.

Take Profit:

- Set take-profit targets for both positions to lock in your gains when the correlation between the currency pairs starts to break down.

- Take-profit levels should be based on your profit objectives and risk tolerance.

Appropriate Pair:

- Choose currency pairs with a strong and stable historical correlation.

- Consider pairs that move in the same direction most of the time and have a correlation coefficient close to 1 or -1.

Timing:

- Implement this strategy during periods of market stability and avoid highly volatile market conditions.

- Watch for potential shifts in market sentiment or economic data releases that may impact the correlation between the currency pairs.

| 44. MOMENTUM TRADING WITH MULTIPLE TIMEFRAMES

| Use multiple momentum indicators with different periods to identify potential trading opportunities. | Can be profitable in trending markets. | Momentum indicators can be lagging, can be whipsawed in choppy markets. | 1-2% of account | 2-3 ATR | 1-2 ATR | Any pair | During strong trends |

Momentum trading is a strategy that involves identifying and trading stocks or currency pairs that are trending. The idea is to buy stocks or currency pairs that are moving up in price and sell stocks or currency pairs that are moving down in price.

One way to identify trending stocks or currency pairs is to use momentum indicators. Momentum indicators measure the rate of change of a stock or currency pair's price. A rising momentum indicator suggests that the stock or currency pair is trending up, while a falling momentum indicator suggests that the stock or currency pair is trending down.

There are many different momentum indicators that traders can use. Some of the most popular momentum indicators include:

Relative Strength Index (RSI): The RSI measures the ratio of a stock or currency pair's recent gains to its recent losses. An

RSI value above 70 indicates that the stock or currency pair is overbought, while an RSI value below 30 indicates that the stock or currency pair is oversold.

Stochastic Oscillator: The Stochastic Oscillator measures the relationship between a stock or currency pair's closing price and its high and low prices over a given period of time. A Stochastic Oscillator value above 80 indicates that the stock or currency pair is overbought, while a Stochastic Oscillator value below 20 indicates that the stock or currency pair is oversold.

Moving Average Convergence Divergence (MACD): The MACD is a trend-following indicator that compares a stock or currency pair's short-term moving average to its long-term moving average. A rising MACD indicates that the stock or currency pair is trending up, while a falling MACD indicates that the stock or currency pair is trending down.

How to Use Momentum Trading with Multiple Timeframes

Momentum trading with multiple timeframes involves using momentum indicators with different periods to identify potential trading opportunities. For example, a trader might use a short-term momentum indicator, such as the RSI, to identify stocks or currency pairs that are trending up in the short term. The trader might then use a long-term momentum indicator, such as the MACD, to identify stocks or currency pairs that are trending up in the long term.

When a trader identifies a stock or currency pair that is trending up on both the short-term and long-term timeframes, the trader can enter a long position. The trader can then place a stop-loss order below the stock or currency pair's recent low to protect their profits.

Pros And Cons Of Momentum Trading With Multiple Timeframes

Momentum trading with multiple timeframes can be a profitable strategy, but it also has some risks.

Pros:

Can be profitable in trending markets.

Relatively easy to understand and implement.

Can be used to trade stocks, currency pairs, and other financial instruments.

Cons:

Momentum indicators can be lagging, meaning they can take some time to confirm a trend.

Momentum indicators can be whipsawed in choppy markets, leading to false signals.

Momentum trading can be risky, especially if a trader uses too much leverage.

Risk Management

Risk management is an important part of any trading strategy, and momentum trading is no exception. Traders should always use stop-loss orders to protect their profits and limit their losses. Traders should also be aware of the risks of overtrading and should only trade with a portion of their account balance.

Note

Momentum trading with multiple timeframes can be a profitable strategy, but it is important to be aware of the risks involved. Traders should always use stop-loss orders and should only trade with a portion of their account balance.

| 45. NEWS TRADING WITH MULTIPLE SOURCES

| Use multiple news sources to identify potential trading opportunities. | Can be profitable if you can get the news before the market does. | News events can be difficult to predict, can be whipsawed by false news. | 1-2% of account | 2-3 ATR | 1-2 ATR | Any pair | News events |

This strategy involves utilizing multiple news sources to identify potential trading opportunities. The goal is to capitalize on market movements caused by news events before they are fully priced into the market. By monitoring news feeds and analyzing market reactions, traders can seek to profit from short-term price fluctuations.

Key Points:

Multiple News Sources: News trading requires access to real-time news feeds from various sources, including reputable financial news agencies, social media platforms, and economic calendars. Traders should strive to gather information from diverse sources to ensure they have a comprehensive understanding of market-moving events.

Identifying Trading Opportunities: News events can have a significant impact on currency pairs, stocks, and other financial instruments. Traders should focus on news events with the potential to cause substantial market volatility, such as economic data releases, central bank announcements, political developments, or natural disasters.

Market Reaction Analysis: Once a news event occurs, traders should analyze the initial market reaction to gauge its significance and potential impact. This involves monitoring price movements, order flow, and market sentiment. If the news is perceived as positive, prices may rise; if negative, prices may fall.

Trading Execution: Traders should act quickly to capitalize on news-driven price movements. This may involve placing buy or sell orders immediately following the news release or adjusting existing positions to align with the anticipated market direction. Speed and precision are crucial in executing news trades.

Risk Management: News trading carries a high degree of risk due to the unpredictable nature of news events and the potential for false or misleading information. Traders should implement strict risk management measures, such as setting appropriate stop-loss orders and limiting their exposure to a single news event.

Advantages:

Profit Potential: News trading can be highly profitable if traders can accurately anticipate market reactions to news events and execute trades swiftly.

Short-Term Opportunities: News-driven price movements often present short-term trading opportunities, allowing traders to capture quick profits.

Disadvantages:

Unpredictability: News events are inherently unpredictable, making it challenging to forecast market reactions with certainty.

False News: Traders may fall victim to false or misleading news reports, leading to incorrect trading decisions.

Whipsaw Risk: Markets can experience sudden reversals following news events, resulting in losses for traders who hold positions in the wrong direction.

Recommended Parameters:

Account Size: 1-2% of the account balance should be allocated to each trade.

Stop-Loss: Place stop-loss orders within 2-3 ATR (Average True Range) of the entry price to limit potential losses.

Take-Profit: Target take-profit levels should be set within 1-2 ATR of the entry price to maximize profit potential.

Currency Pairs: This strategy can be applied to any currency pair, but it is often most effective for highly liquid pairs with significant news-driven volatility.

Trading Time: News trading is best suited for periods when significant news events are expected, such as during economic data releases or major political announcements.

Indeed, news trading with multiple sources can be a rewarding strategy for experienced traders who can effectively manage risk and execute trades based on real-time news updates. However, beginners should approach this strategy with caution due to its inherent volatility and potential for substantial losses.

| 46. SENTIMENT TRADING WITH MULTIPLE INDICATORS

| Use multiple sentiment indicators to gauge market sentiment. | Can be profitable if you can accurately gauge market sentiment. | Market sentiment can be difficult to measure, can be whipsawed by sudden changes in sentiment. | 1-2% of account | 2-3 ATR | 1-2 ATR | Any pair | Periods of strong sentiment |

Sentiment trading is a strategy that involves using multiple indicators to measure how the market feels about a certain pair. Some of the indicators that can be used are the Commitment of Traders report, the VIX index, the put/call ratio, and the sentiment surveys. By using these indicators, you can get a sense of whether the market is bullish or bearish, and trade accordingly. For example, if the indicators show that the market is overly bullish, you can look for opportunities to sell, and vice versa. This strategy can be profitable if you can accurately gauge market sentiment and catch the major trends. However, it also has some drawbacks. Market sentiment can be difficult to measure, and it can change quickly due to unexpected events or news. This can lead to false signals or whipsaws, where the market reverses direction suddenly. To avoid this, you should use other tools such as price action, trend lines, and support and resistance levels to confirm your sentiment signals. You should also use proper risk management and position sizing. A good rule of thumb is to risk only 1-2% of your account per trade, and use a stop loss of 2-3 ATR below or above your entry point. Your profit target should be at least 1-2 ATR away from your entry point, or you can use a trailing stop to lock in profits. You can apply this strategy to any pair, but it works best in periods of strong sentiment, where the market is clearly moving in one direction.

| 47. PATTERN TRADING WITH MULTIPLE PATTERNS

| Use multiple chart patterns to identify potential trading opportunities. | Can be profitable if you can accurately identify chart patterns. | Chart patterns can be subjective, can be broken in volatile markets. | 1-2% of account | 2-3 ATR | 1-2 ATR | Any pair | When chart patterns are forming |

One of the ways to trade the forex market is to use multiple chart patterns. Chart patterns are geometric shapes that form on the price charts and indicate the direction of the market. Some of the common chart patterns are triangles, flags, wedges, head and shoulders, double tops and bottoms, etc.

Trading with multiple chart patterns can be profitable if you can accurately identify them and follow the rules of entry, exit and risk management. For example, you can use a triangle pattern to enter a breakout trade, and then use a flag pattern to add to your position or take partial profits. You can also use chart patterns to set your stop loss and take profit levels based on the size of the pattern or the projected target.

However, trading with multiple chart patterns also has some challenges and risks. Chart patterns can be subjective, meaning that different traders may see different patterns on the same chart. Chart patterns can also be broken or invalidated by sudden price movements in volatile markets. Therefore, you need to be careful and flexible when trading with multiple chart patterns.

A Possible Strategy For Trading With Multiple Chart Patterns Is As Follows

- Risk only 1-2% of your account per trade.

- Use 2-3 ATR (average true range) as your stop loss level.

- Use 1-2 ATR as your take profit level.

- Trade any currency pair that shows clear chart patterns.

- Trade when chart patterns are forming or completed, depending on your preference and risk tolerance.

| 48. SCALPING WITH MULTIPLE CURRENCY PAIRS

| Scalp multiple currency pairs simultaneously. | Can be profitable in volatile markets. | Requires fast reaction times, can be stressful. | 0.5-1% of account | 10-20 pips | 10-20 pips | Volatile pairs, e.g., EUR/USD, GBP/USD | High volatility periods |

Scalping is a trading strategy that involves opening and closing positions in multiple currency pairs simultaneously, aiming to profit from small price movements. Scalpers typically use high leverage and trade during periods of high volatility, such as the London and New York sessions. Scalping can be profitable in volatile markets, as it allows traders to exploit short-term fluctuations and capture multiple profits. However, scalping also requires fast reaction times, as the market can change quickly and unpredictably. Scalpers need to monitor their positions closely and exit them as soon as they reach their target or stop loss. Scalping can be stressful and demanding, as it requires constant attention and discipline. Scalpers usually risk 0.5-1% of their account per trade and aim for 10-20 pips of profit or loss. They also need to consider the spread and commission costs, which can eat into their profits. Scalpers tend to trade volatile pairs, such as EUR/USD and GBP/USD, as they offer more opportunities for price movements. They also look for high volatility periods, such as news releases, economic data, and market open/close times, as they can trigger large price swings.

| 49. DAY TRADING WITH MULTIPLE STRATEGIES

| Use multiple trading strategies simultaneously. | Can be profitable if the strategies are complementary. | Requires a lot of time and attention, can be stressful. | 1-2% of account | 2-3 ATR | 1-2 ATR | Any pair | During the day |

Day trading with multiple strategies can be a profitable way to trade the financial markets. However, it is important to note that this strategy is not without its risks. It is important to have a good understanding of each strategy that you are using and to be able to trade them effectively. Additionally, it is important to have a risk management plan in place to protect your capital.

One of the benefits of day trading with multiple strategies is that it can help to diversify your risk. If one strategy is not performing well, you can still make money with the other strategies. Additionally, using multiple strategies can help you to identify market trends more effectively.

However, day trading with multiple strategies can also be more time-consuming and stressful than using a single strategy. It is important to be able to manage your time effectively and to be able to trade without getting emotional.

Here Are Some Tips For Day Trading With Multiple Strategies:

Chose strategies that are complementary. This means that the strategies should not overlap too much. For example, you could use a trend following strategy and a mean reversion strategy.

Have a good understanding of each strategy. You should know how each strategy works and how to trade it effectively.

Use a risk management plan. This will help you to protect your capital and to limit your losses.

Be patient. It takes time to learn how to trade multiple strategies effectively. Don't get discouraged if you don't see results immediately.

Day trading with multiple strategies can be a profitable way to trade the financial markets. However, it is important to have a good understanding of the risks involved and to be able to trade the strategies effectively.

| 50. POSITION TRADING WITH MULTIPLE TIMEFRAMES

| Use multiple timeframes to identify the overall trend and then trade in the direction of that trend on a longer timeframe. | Can be profitable in trending markets. | Requires patience, can be difficult to identify the overall trend. | 5-10% of account | 5-10 ATR | 5-10 ATR | Trending pairs, e.g., EUR/USD, GBP/USD | Long-term trends |

Position Trading With Multiple Timeframes: A Comprehensive Exploration

Position trading with multiple timeframes is a strategic approach in the financial markets that involves analyzing price action across different timeframes to identify long-term trends and execute trades accordingly.

Key Elements Of The Strategy

1. Trend Identification:

   - Analyze multiple timeframes, typically ranging from daily to weekly or even monthly charts, to identify the overall trend of an asset.

- Look for consistent patterns, such as higher highs and higher lows in an uptrend or lower highs and lower lows in a downtrend.

2. Trade Execution:

- Once a clear trend is identified, focus on trading in the direction of that trend on a longer timeframe.

- Enter trades that align with the identified trend, typically aiming for long-term profitability.

3. Patience and Discipline:

- Position trading requires patience as trends can take a while to develop and materialize.

- Traders need to be disciplined in sticking to their strategy and not making impulsive trades.

4. Risk Management:

- Use sound risk management techniques, such as stop-loss orders and position sizing, to protect capital in case of unexpected market movements.

5. Trading Parameters:

- Allocate 5-10% of the trading account to each position.

- Set stop-loss orders 5-10 ATR (Average True Range) away from the entry price.

- Take profit targets 5-10 ATR away from the entry price.

6. Suitable Pairs and Trends:

- Identify trending currency pairs that exhibit long-term trends, such as EUR/USD, GBP/USD, or other major pairs.

- Focus on longer-term trends, such as those lasting for several months or even years.

Examples of Position Trading Execution:

- Uptrend Identification: Analyze weekly and monthly charts to identify a bullish trend in EUR/USD.

- Entry: Wait for a pullback within the uptrend and enter a long position with a stop-loss below the pullback low.

- Target: Set a profit target in line with the identified trend, allowing the trade to run until the trend shows signs of reversal.

Benefits:

- Can be profitable in trending markets.

- Offers the potential for substantial gains if the trend continues.

- Helps to avoid short-term market noise and focus on the long-term direction.

Challenges:

- Requires patience and discipline, as trends can take a while to develop.

- Difficult to identify the overall trend, especially for beginners.

- Not suitable for short-term traders who prefer quick profits.

Indeed, position trading with multiple timeframes involves identifying long-term trends and trading in the direction of those trends on longer timeframes. This approach requires patience, sound risk management, and the ability to recognize and capitalize on long-term market opportunities.

GLOSSARY

Ask price: The price at which a seller is willing to sell a currency pair.

Bid price: The price at which a buyer is willing to buy a currency pair.

Currency pair: Two currencies that are traded against each other, such as EUR/USD or GBP/JPY.

Foreign exchange (Forex): The market for trading currencies.

Forex broker: A company that provides a platform for traders to buy and sell currencies.

Leverage: The use of borrowed money to increase the size of a trade.

Lot: A standard unit of currency trading, typically 100,000 units of the base currency.

Margin: The amount of money required to open and maintain a leveraged trade.

Pip: The smallest unit of change in a currency pair's price.

Spread: The difference between the ask price and the bid price.

Stop loss order: An order that automatically closes a trade when the price reaches a certain level, limiting the trader's losses.

Take profit order: An order that automatically closes a trade when the price reaches a certain level, locking in the trader's profits.

Finally, Let's Explain How Each Of The Following

Indicator Is Applied In Forex Trading:

Moving average: A technical indicator that shows the average price of a currency pair over a specified period of time.

Relative strength index (RSI): A technical indicator that measures the strength of a trend by comparing the average gain of a currency pair to its average loss.

Stochastic oscillator: A technical indicator that measures the momentum of a currency pair by comparing the current price to the highest and lowest prices over a specified period of time.

Bollinger bands: A technical indicator that shows the upper and lower limits of a currency pair's price movement over a specified period of time.

Ichimoku cloud: A technical indicator that shows the trend, momentum, and support and resistance levels of a currency pair.

Fibonacci retracement levels: A technical indicator that shows the potential retracement levels of a currency pair after a significant move.

Support and resistance levels: Price levels at which a currency pair tends to bounce off of.

Moving Average:

- Moving averages are applied in Forex trading to identify the overall trend of a currency pair and to smooth out price fluctuations.

- Traders can use moving averages to determine potential entry and exit points for trades.

- A currency pair that is trading above its moving average is generally considered to be in an uptrend, while a currency pair that is trading below its moving average is generally considered to be in a downtrend.

Relative Strength Index (RSI):

- The RSI is applied in Forex trading to measure the strength of a trend and to identify potential overbought or oversold conditions.
- An RSI reading above 70 generally indicates that a currency pair is overbought and may be due for a correction, while an RSI reading below 30 generally indicates that a currency pair is oversold and may be due for a rally.

Stochastic Oscillator:

- The stochastic oscillator is applied in Forex trading to measure the momentum of a currency pair and to identify potential turning points in the market.
- The stochastic oscillator consists of two lines, the %K line and the %D line.
- When the %K line crosses above the %D line, it generally indicates that the currency pair is gaining momentum and may be due for a rally.
- When the %K line crosses below the %D line, it generally indicates that the currency pair is losing momentum and may be due for a correction.

Bollinger Bands:

- Bollinger bands are applied in Forex trading to identify potential areas of support and resistance and to measure the volatility of a currency pair.
- Bollinger bands consist of three lines, the upper Bollinger band, the middle Bollinger band, and the lower Bollinger band.
- The middle Bollinger band is a simple moving average of the currency pair's price, while the upper and lower Bollinger bands are set a specified number of standard deviations above and

below the middle Bollinger band.

- When the currency pair's price is trading above the upper Bollinger band, it generally indicates that the pair is overbought and may be due for a correction.

- When the currency pair's price is trading below the lower Bollinger band, it generally indicates that the pair is oversold and may be due for a rally.

Ichimoku Cloud:

- The Ichimoku cloud is applied in Forex trading to identify the trend, momentum, and support and resistance levels of a currency pair.

- The Ichimoku cloud consists of five lines, the Tenkan-sen, the Kijun-sen, the Senkou Span A, the Senkou Span B, and the Chikou Span.

- The Tenkan-sen and Kijun-sen lines are used to identify the trend of the currency pair.

- The Senkou Span A and Senkou Span B lines are used to identify potential areas of support and resistance.

- The Chikou Span is used to identify potential turning points in the market.

Fibonacci Retracement Levels:

- Fibonacci retracement levels are applied in Forex trading to identify potential retracement levels of a currency pair after a significant move.

- Fibonacci retracement levels are based on the Fibonacci sequence, a series of numbers in which each number is the sum of the two previous numbers.

- The most common Fibonacci retracement levels are 23.6%, 38.2%, 50%, 61.8%, and 78.6%.

- Traders can use Fibonacci retracement levels to identify

potential areas to place stop-loss orders or take-profit orders.

Support and Resistance Levels:

- Support and resistance levels are applied in Forex trading to identify areas where the currency pair's price is likely to bounce off of.
- Support levels are areas where the currency pair's price has previously found buyers, while resistance levels are areas where the currency pair's price has previously found sellers.
- Traders can use support and resistance levels to identify potential areas to enter and exit trades.

Thanks for reading. And don't forget to take breaks, eat, and get some sleep. Confused? Any strategy can lead to profit if you stay consistent. Read again the section on moving averages. Make small tweeks, if needed, until you in fall in love with your strategy. A single digit makes a big difference. Small profit of 1 percent or more? Take it.

Alfonso Borello, February 2024